CONVERSATIONS WITH WOMEN IN MUSIC PRODUCTION

CONVERSATIONS WITH WOMEN IN MUSIC PRODUCTION

The Interviews

Kallie Marie

Backbeat
Books

Essex, Connecticut

An imprint of Globe Pequot, the trade division of
The Rowman & Littlefield Publishing Group, Inc.
4501 Forbes Blvd., Ste. 200
Lanham, MD 20706
www.rowman.com

Distributed by NATIONAL BOOK NETWORK

British Library Cataloguing in Publication Information available

Library of Congress Cataloging-in-Publication Data

Names: Marie, Kallie, 1980– interviewer, author.
Title: Conversations with women in music production : the interviews /
  Kallie Marie.
Description: Guilford, Connecticut : Backbeat, 2022. | Includes
  bibliographical references.
Identifiers: LCCN 2021054961 (print) | LCCN 2021054962 (ebook) | ISBN
  9781493065066 (paperback) | ISBN 9781493065073 (epub)
Subjects: LCSH: Women sound recording executives and producers—Interviews.
  | Women sound engineers—Interviews. | Sound recording industry.
Classification: LCC ML82 .C68 2022 (print) | LCC ML82 (ebook) | DDC
  780.82—dc23
LC record available at https://lccn.loc.gov/2021054961
LC ebook record available at https://lccn.loc.gov/2021054962

CONTENTS

FOREWORD

Methodology and the Interviewees

In 2016, when this research started, there was very little academic writing on the psychological, socioeconomic, and shared lived experiences of women functioning and succeeding (and in some cases struggling) within a very specific microcosm of the recording industry. During this research, I focused specifically on recording engineers and record producers. The term *producer* is used here in the traditional sense and not as it is used today, to encompass anyone who utilizes software to work on music or who has some means of production to produce their own work. Here the term delineates a person hired by either a studio, an artist or band, or a label to work on the production aspects of the music (including but not limited to the stages of preproduction, production, and sometimes extends to postproduction) and help oversee and guide the creative and technical aspects of music production as a whole.

(You will see that I do not include live sound engineers, mix engineers, mastering engineers, DJs, or self-stylized and self-producing artists on the whole. There may be more or fewer women and gender minorities in some of these professional spaces than in others. Although one or two producers interviewed here may also be music makers and artists and there are in some cases a crossover with self-producing artists, theirs is a different set of unique challenges. These I believe to have their own professional circumstances that present too broad a topic to address adequately within this work. My exclusion of these other career pathways allows me to focus on aspects specific to recording engineers, record producers, and audio engineers, like the ability to sell oneself to an artist, to thrive in networking situations, and to prove technical prowess.)

This work emerged initially at the behest of some of my colleagues and mentors who had asked me to write specifically on this area, with women as the focus. I had to think long and hard about the undercurrents that at that time seemed to still hold some people back professionally while exploring how success had been possible for others. The summation of what I had uncovered was published as a chapter in a different book. Since then, the topic and the surrounding conversations have greatly evolved. The research itself, both in conducting the interviews and the time it took to transcribe them, spanned a year or two. During this time, a lot changed in the music industry and the world. Initially, my aims had been pointed: I had wanted to curate conversations exploring the experiences of women who were noticeably at peak places in their careers and who had been working in recording engineering and music production for at least a decade or more. I wanted to be as diverse and as inclusive as possible, including as many different perspectives as I had access to at the time. I had hoped to uncover the parameters of overt and covert sexism in society and its impact on these women's careers within the recording industry and, to no lesser extent, the effect this had on the music that they made or were kept from making. I wanted to hear their reflections and views, and from as many backgrounds and demographics as possible.

I was mindful to not present a body of research that was merely—as some might deride it—"women complaining," which as a societal construct is already a strong detractor narrative, and I didn't want to have to climb over that narrative in order to get to a set of discussions that are worthy of being heard. Instead, I outlined a few topics, presenting the experiences of the structures of the recording industry as these engineers and producers view them, and give voice to where they believe the challenges still lie and how we might look to overcome them as we move forward.

I was also hoping to uncover some insights into whether the women working in the field with whom I spoke were experiencing the same things and, if not, what differences they were experiencing and why.

What were the parallels? Were there any patterns? The comparative stories of these producers and engineers show some similar experiences and coping mechanisms. It is perhaps quite telling that many of the people I spoke with often referred to themselves as uniquely singular, or, in other words, alone and unlike anyone else. This sense of being othered is mentioned many times throughout our conversations. One may start to wonder, "What is the impact on a person's work, output, and personal life if they frequently view themselves as other or an outsider?" In some cases, I suspect some of the women I spoke with have made their "difference" a point of pride, while others perhaps tried to shy away from it and not draw attention to the fact that they are women. I explore this briefly with them by bringing up *stereotype threat*, a term unfamiliar to most of the people I interviewed, which refers to the cognitive toll a person subconsciously experiences that often leads to poorer performance when that person is aware of being part of a stereotype or stereotyped group.

Society's attitudes about women's assumed demeanor, the *politeness perception*, as I've termed it, relates to and influences these women's experiences with technology, negotiations for and around childcare, pay equity, and experiences of early childhood socialization and education, which have all played a role in how their careers took shape. The conversations were carefully curated over the course of the interviews presented here. Sometimes it was tricky to initiate a topic, which first required some trust building. It did seem at times that many of the women were uncomfortable talking about certain subjects in particular. Some of them warmed up a little as I shared my experiences too, and so in certain instances readers will see our conversation deviate briefly to share some of my own personal experiences, giving us a chance to expand and explore more conversationally where relevant. I, too, am a recording engineer and producer, of about twenty years (as of this writing), which has informed my writing on this topic and the conversations herein. A lot of these shared experiences were personally relatable, which enriched our exchanges. The *how* of the path, the *why* of the roadblocks, and the mechanics of existing in these spaces uncover a map of their intricate journeys, presented here for the reader's consideration. Each of these women has carved out a successful career in recording and/or music production while navigating a juxtaposition of identity, overcoming societal biases, and balancing their own career progress and confidence in their work, more so at some times than at others.

Aside from highlighting the remaining issues, it was also important to shed light on why they feel that this is an important conversation or not, their thoughts on the future, and how they view the hurdles that remain and possible solutions to them. There can be no one simple answer to the complex set of questions that I put to them, and I didn't anticipate that one person or group of people could sum up such varied experiences, social norms, and societal issues. Rather, I posed new questions to well-respected industry veterans, highlighting and questioning some of the more ingrained nuances of societal biases, asking them to share their views, their experiences, and their ideas on potential solutions.

It is no longer sufficient to highlight that there are problems in the industry, present statistics about how few women work in it, and hope for the best. Rather, it is important to have difficult discussions that evoke complex answers, reflecting on the industry and our society, and then consider what possible solutions look like and how they can be implemented, which are valuable vantage points to operate from. Increasing initiatives to educate girls more equally in STEM (science, technology, engineering, and mathematics) and its crossover with the arts, STEAM, and increasing the visibility of women and gender minorities are wonderful first steps. However, what happens when they get into the workforce? To that end, we must consider the women who made it without the aforementioned benefits: How did they do it? How do they view their experiences? What insights can they offer? Without having these conversations, there's no way of knowing what new approaches are needed and what steps can be taken to try out these different approaches, open mindsets, and, hopefully, open some doors.

It was my wish to make the roster of women I interviewed as diverse as possible; regrettably, some key engineers and producers in the trans and queer community I had reached out to did not wish to participate in this discussion, but they were definitely intended to be here. It is my hope that if there are future expansions of this research I can add their voices and insights to this work. A surprising number of successful engineers also opted out of this conversation, which was telling in and of itself. I found it very hard to get some people to open up about their experiences, and perhaps the reader will find some insight in reading between the lines in a few responses. It is also interesting to note that many people I contacted refused my interview request and even emailed back, saying, "I wouldn't touch this subject with a ten-foot pole." Moreover, and equally telling, some who did speak with me wished to remain anonymous for fear of harming their careers, and others backed out at the last minute because they didn't want to go on record as a woman talking about these topics for fear of alienating peers or losing work. I deeply empathize with their reticence, as I myself have had my own misgivings about writing on this topic, wondering how doing so may impact my own recording, producing, and composing career going forward.

This research, at the end of the day, is intended to highlight all of these engineers' and producers' lived experiences and their own feelings about them. It is a curated conversation, and each person will have their own views, experiences, and feelings about these topics, based on their own demographics and unique life experiences. Their differing perspectives were equally valuable, while it was interesting to see the many commonalities in their experiences emerge.

The focus of the questions is outlined by chapter. The categories were, in most cases, announced to the interviewees as we progressed through the conversation. In some cases, interviewees refused comment on specific questions, and others were never comfortable openly discussing certain topics on the record, later sending me messages explaining that they hadn't disclosed half of what they would have liked to. It is here that different kinds of silence are meaningful. Silence can still speak volumes, but those stories are not for me to share. However, it is worth consideration, as the ways women and minorities are silenced are telling. Author and activist Rebecca Solnit has dedicated an entire book to discussions on this topic, and here her words are poignant in the context of our discussions in this book.

> Who is heard and who is not defines the status quo. Those who embody it, often at the cost of extraordinary silences with themselves, move to the center; those who embody what is not heard or what violates those who rise on silence are cast out. By redefining whose voice is valued, we redefine our society and its values . . . that subspecies of silence and silencing specific to women, if anything can be specific to more than half of humanity. If to have a voice, to be allowed to speak, to be heard and believed is essential to being an insider or person of power, a human being with full membership, then it's important to recognize that silence is the universal condition of oppression, and there are many kinds of silence and of the silenced. (Solnit 2017, 24)

I had hoped to give these engineers and producers a chance to explore some concepts and perhaps reflect on things in ways they may not yet have had the chance to previously, or to share their stories in ways that they felt valuable and authentic to themselves. Our conversations became an opportunity to see everyone's experiences side by side, which can help others realize that, no, they're not imagining things, they are *not* being too sensitive, it is not all in their head, and it is not their fault. It was jarring to see in the interviews just how internalized a lot of things were for some of the interviewees, perhaps reflective of their demographic or personality or maybe forged as a coping mechanism. I have done my best to present the interviews as they occurred and leave their words to the interpretation of the reader. All viewpoints and perspectives are valuable, for together they show a fuller picture. After all, these are their experiences, and we can learn much from them.

I invite the reader to reflect deeply on their own attitudes, internalizations, and societal normalizations of prevalent attitudes and beliefs. Chiefly an attitude that women's brains are different and less technical and not capable of scientific work underpins the subtle sexism pervasive today. This view is increasingly disproven among the scientific community. Substantial research shows that aptitudes in STEM and STEAM are related to early childhood development, nurture, and education, and not to gender, as had once been assumed. I would point readers with an interest in exploring this to the work of scholars like Cordelia Fine, whose research on social cognition and neuroscience earned 2017's Royal Society Insight Investment Science Book Prize and has informed much of my research.

In closing, if speaking about your professional experiences could cost you your career, then we have identified a conversation we should be having not just within one industry but as a society. This is a neon sign that things are not equal. If women are saying that they hoped no one at work would notice they are a woman, then there's a problem. On the whole, men generally don't go to work saying, "I hope no one notices I am a man." Although similar and complex feelings for men working in childcare might be the closest parallel, their experiences are still shaped differently by our collective societal views on the gendered capabilities of men.

While I have only begun to scratch the surface with these conversations, and through them identify some of the as-of-yet unresolved issues both in the recording industry and society at large, along with highlighting the shared experiences, both positive and negative, we can better understand the patterns and mindsets that shape so much of the industry, music, and, ultimately, people's lives and careers. The voices here are various and unique. I hope readers absorb these candid conversations slowly and evaluate their insights deeply. We have work to do still, and it will benefit all of us and may shape music in ways we cannot yet fathom.

1

GENDERED PERCEPTIONS INFLUENCING THE RECORD-MAKING PROCESS

The experiences of the engineers and producers discussed in this book span a few decades and include the periods before the major technological advances to the present day. Some of the women interviewed have worked during the older music industry model of large multinational corporate major record labels with big-budget-style productions in an era before streaming. Others mentioned that they were just coming up, as I did, when this was starting to shift; the Internet was in its early stages, major label monopolies were beginning to break up, and independent labels were becoming more prominent. Notable, too, would be key technological inventions underpinning a lot of these changes for the engineers and producers interviewed (which is discussed in further detail in a later chapter about technological accessibility as a potential democratizer); the first digital audio workstations (DAWs) and some of the moves away from the traditional studio hierarchies were in their early stages during this period. We see the first instances of "home studios," as well as innovations like plug-ins and more powerful computers, emerge during this time. In hindsight, these technological advances have really changed the way music is made. For example, in 2004, a 250 GB portable HD with a 7200 RPM was heavy and quite large (by today's standards); it needed external power and was pretty expensive.

(I now have a 2TB flash drive sitting on my desk, the size of a standard USB drive and at a fraction of the cost of the aforementioned drive of yore. I am sure within just a few years of writing this, things will have advanced even further and faster.) So while the landscape of music making has evolved from the process of thirty to forty years ago, for those working today, these previous paradigms cast a long shadow. Working nearly from a musicological framework for this first chapter, the analytic structure and line of questioning were devised to look at recording industry paradigms that have recently started to shift.

While women's experiences of these shifts are explored in more depth later, it is important to start with what they had experienced initially (if they were active in their careers during the earlier paradigm) or of the remaining overhang from the previous paradigm model, which is rapidly being reshaped by things like social media, online streaming, and other avenues of revenue for everyone in music and music production globally. During the pandemic of 2020–2022, these changes, to things like who controls popularity and who gets to make records, became more visible. That is not to say that major labels don't hold any sway; in a very large way, they still dominate what gets played on the radio and major streaming services like Spotify—and who gets paid from these streams. (Under the current model, major labels, for example, collect the royalties and then redistribute them among their artists based on popularity, often leaving independent artists without their fair share or their royalties lost and not distributed at all.) A recent *Rolling Stone* article summed it up best: "Spotify pays out its royalties on a pro-rata basis, meaning that, at the end of each accounting period, all of its royalty money gets virtually dumped into one pot, from which artists are paid according to their share of all streams on the platform. So if a group of artists is getting 90% of the streams, they're also getting 90% of the money" (Ingham 2020) Without diving headlong into how those systems work, notably, major labels are also major shareholders in Spotify, for example, and do control how black box monies are distributed. Nevertheless, many new artists are surfacing and discovering ways to skip over gatekeepers and find their audiences—forcing the major players to take note.

The *audible male gaze*, my term to describe what we as a society (or perhaps formerly as major labels) deem acceptable for the kinds of music women make or are assumed capable of making or are marketable enough to make. This includes the kinds of women who get to make music and be visible and what they get to make and perform music about, which is something that we begin to explore in this chapter of questions. The audible male gaze is more prevalent in some music genres than others, especially in pop music. One need only to think about the harsh critiques heaved at Madonna for suddenly being too old or at extremely young Billie Eilish for being a different body shape than what is preferred (by whom?). Again, pop music is harsher on women and women-identifying people, where ageism is also at play. For example, women aren't allowed to age in nearly the same way as their male counterparts are, and their product (i.e., music) is deemed less viable or marketable. Tori Amos talked openly with Ann Powers in their book *Piece by Piece* about an incident with Atlantic Records in 1998, when they planned to bury her and not promote her work because she was considered too old:

> "Tori, wake up. It's over." Silence. "What?" "They won." "What" I said in shock, in walking nightmare kind of voice. "They won. They've got you sewn up for three records. I'm sorry, I'm so sorry, Tor. I think they want to bury you." "How can they bury me?" I said, somewhat dazed. "I can play a full house at Madison Square Garden with or without Atlantic." "Yes, but they've got you sewn up for three records and by then they say you'll be . . ." "What, be what?" I said, now with tears running down my face in this small café, with the waiters bringing me napkins for the dam that was about to burst. "Be what?" I whispered, through the tears. He lowered his voice and said,

"Oh, honey—too old. And then . . ." "And then, what?" I demanded. "And then no one will want you."

Rock music and all its subgenres have a different set of constraints; for example, in rock, punk, and metal, we don't see women having the massive successes of Alice Cooper, Green Day, or Metallica, performing in those styles. Because these "harsher/tougher" genres of music are seen as less feminine, the women in these styles have to put on a different bravado (perhaps in some ways overcompensating, even if they identify with the subculture of that genre) to fit in, or they get left out; they may be more free in terms of visual imagery under the old paradigm models, but *free* in this case is a loose term and really depends on the artistic vision of the creator and the production team. Without digressing into a completely different discussion of cultural underpinnings, these points are part of the undercurrent of my questioning during this chapter. What music doesn't get made? How does this audible male gaze affect the music that gets a budget, gets signed, or gets promoted (nevermind how)? That is a much larger question than can be addressed here, so what I asked these women is how they experienced these influences and their thoughts on them. There are some cultural parallels here; for example, in pro league sports, it's argued that women's teams aren't as marketable for a variety of reasons. Similarly, what are some of the subconscious biases that are held about how women shouldn't sound, behave, or write in these music genres? Western society seems to have plenty of time for music by women to be in one of two camps: "sexy diva" or "mournful siren," especially in pop but not limited to it. It's almost like a lot of music considered the standard "chick music" would fail its own Bechdel test. That is not to say that there aren't exceptions; there very often are. The focus here is on what upholds these stereotypes and whether they hold anyone back. Another parallel is any sampling of women's Halloween costumes in the United States. Most of the costumes are "Sexy_____," and whatever it is it had better be sexy.

Again, this is not to say that it is wrong to be sexy or that it isn't popular and doesn't sell. The important notion here is: Does the audible male gaze limit people in this context and, if so, how? Is music constrained by this audible male gaze? This topic alone could be its own discourse for a body of research, perhaps too broad for the scope of this book.

Additionally, some women interviewed had no major label experiences, while others did. We discussed the paradigm shifts and what they feel its impact is, before moving on to talking about recent developments to the industry. This is when the 1990s Lilith Fair and "girl power" branding emerged in some genres of music. This branding had a different set of semiotic coding and complexities, resulting in a different style of othering for women making music. These types of labels sought to communicate that the music was "women's music" or "chick music" or a "chick band" and somehow was not for everyone (i.e., men). I wondered if these women felt pushed out from making certain kinds of music or if they had a self awareness in making sure they didn't get labeled as making "chick music." While most were not performers themselves, I wanted to know what they had seen from their side of the glass and if there had been artists they fought to get recorded or projects they believed in that received pushback.

Focusing on "chick music" and the *assumed feminine touch,* my term for the subconscious bias that women make pretty, soft, elegant, or sexy music—in other words, decorative or titillating but not serious—that music is somehow gendered from the outset. There is plenty of writing on these musicological topics, so the intent isn't to unpack those here but to look at how these subconscious biases may impact what music gets made and if these women were deemed capable of recording and producing music that wasn't "women's music" or "chick music."

Were these engineers and producers potentially not getting hired or thought of for some projects because subconscious gendered biases can exclude women from certain scenarios or subcultures? In essence: Did the decision-making process and these subconscious biases determine that women were the wrong "culture fit" to make the record? This is perhaps a larger hurdle, depending on the cultural norms associated with a particular style of music. I wanted to find out from these engineers and producers how they had handled working where there might have been perceptions that they couldn't do the "tougher," "harder," or more "technical" style of music. Because many of these women draw from different time periods in the industry and different genres of music, they unsurprisingly had varied experiences. Notably, the women working in rock music developed coping mechanisms (to my own surprise, they were some of the same tactics I employed when I started as a recording engineer and producer, not only because that's the music I liked, but also because I wanted to make sure that no one thought I couldn't make rock records because I was not tough enough [i.e., a woman]). It does, however, raise more questions about presumptions; indeed, Ebonie Smith made a good point about people wanting simply to make records with people they identify with or like hanging out with, and there is no changing that. (There is a large social component to music and music making, and areas like semiotics shed light on how music can be examined under the scope of being, in its own way a unique cultural language with cultural signifiers.) This is indeed a facet of the music industry and is very much why there's a substantial amount of *reading the room* that most engineers and producers do on a daily basis with their clients. Simply put, if you are going to be locked in a room with no windows for twelve hours with someone, you had better hope they're enjoyable to be around. That being said, are women given the chance to be colleagues and not secretaries, groupies, eye candy, and so on? It's more about subverting the expectation of who women can be than it is about a social grouping of who likes hanging with whom because while you must have mutual visions to work together on creative projects, women are too often overlooked and not thought of for roles or are not trusted to be skilled (read technical, which is discussed later) enough to do the work or not seen as an equal one would casually spend time with (which is a larger societal issue). These topics came up in passing with many of the people interviewed here. Abhita Austin and I took a small detour at one point to talk about being misremembered. I've gone to many trade shows and had great interactions with my colleagues about very technical subjects, regarding acoustics, recording, or the gear, and so on, only to have them run into me later and misremember me as a singer (I am *not* a singer), completely forgetting that I am an engineer. Fair dues: We all meet a lot of people, but after repeat renditions of misremembering, as well as finding out that many other women in your field (which is still rare) also experience this same specific misrememberence, one does start to notice a pattern. The act of misremembering someone has a substantial psychological background to it. Angela Saini, in her book *Inferior*, explains,

> American psychologist Diane Ruble and gender development expert Carol Lynn Martin have explained how, by the age of five, children already have in their heads a constellation of gender stereotypes. They describe one experiment in which children were shown pictures of people doing things like sawing and cooking. When a picture contradicted a traditional stereotype, the kids were more likely to remember it incorrectly. In one instance, instead of remembering that they had seen a picture of a girl sawing wood—which they had—someone said instead that they'd seen a boy sawing wood.

It's not surprising, then, that many women recording engineers get misremembered as singers. That's the gendered stereotype, and that's what psychologically gets replaced.

How insidious is this pattern, and how does it affect women when it comes time to figure out whom to hire? Let's try for a second to draw a parallel to another creative industry. Imagine for a moment that you are a film director at some sort of networking event to meet other directors. You meet a woman and talk about doing that job and that role.

The next time you meet her, you ask her how her modeling or acting gig is going—because that's how you view her. She's not your peer, but she might be talent. If she's attractive enough, maybe you can make her a star! Maybe you can discover her!

It is hard to get work if the people in your industry forget you exist because there is such a deeply ingrained cultural assumption that women do not exist in this field and are not technical. Furthermore, even if you claim to be an engineer or producer, you are either misremembered or told that you are not those things, making it even harder to obtain opportunities for work. Try to imagine this happening to men in any field, and it may highlight this strange phenomenon. Are men constantly asked whose boyfriend they are when they try to show up at work?

A personal anecdote of my own to add to these women's stories is an experience I had working with a rock band. More than once I was asked (not by people in the band) by industry people around the band whose girlfriend I was, or I was mistaken for a "party girl." When people are used to seeing women only as potential dates or sometimes as a singer, you practically have to wear a sign around your neck declaring your job, and even still people will file that away with a grain of salt. Sylvia Massy brought up her own experiences that echo this, as did a few other women I spoke with here.

The last point in this chapter is the question, *When is there more than one woman?* This isn't unique to the recording industry. For a start, it's pervasive in many fields and industries, as well as culturally. Two women is too many. We are barely in a place in the United States where we could think of electing a woman for president; furthermore, many would have a hard time digesting a president and a vice president who are both female or identify as female. It's just fine to have two men, though. So this becomes something of an issue in a male-dominated field, where women never see each other. The term *tokenism* comes to mind in some instances. It's deeply isolating, and I wondered how this impacted the output of these engineers and producers. How did they cope? Did they notice? Did they get to work with other women? Some would say, *Why does it matter? Just work with everyone*. Well yes, of course. But that everyone includes women. Ask men how many men they work with in their role, in any role. I am guessing that unless they are a preschool teacher or a nurse (traditional "women's work"), they won't have ever given it a second thought. Psychological studies suggest that stereotype threat sets in and can indeed impact a person's performance on the job. Sadly, a lot of the women I interviewed had never even thought about working with another woman behind the console as engineer and producer or as engineer and second engineer or in any other combination.

I asked the women to reflect on their work environment experiences and how they felt their work environment impacts the music being recorded, their perceptions of clients' responses, and so forth. Many had recorded women but had no experiences with having another woman behind the glass with them. This is evaluated in more detail in a later chapter where stereotype threat is addressed more closely. Interestingly, some women had not reflected on this phenomenon before. For those who had worked with women behind the console, it was because they had hired them.

The impact, apart from the professional and personal experiences of the engineers and producers interviewed, is the music. The music is impacted as a cultural by-product of these institutionalized biases, in the case of the previous paradigms, or in casual subconscious groupings and assumptions about what kinds of music women make. These biases impact the people making the music and the music being made. It's difficult to untangle these categories, as it is a complex relationship between technician, creator, curator, and technology in and among society. In general, the aims of this first chapter are to begin to raise questions about the far-reaching impact that society's biases create by gatekeeping and how this influences who gets to work and what kind of work gets to be done—specifically, music and what kind of music.

TASTEMAKERS AND GATEKEEPERS: THE AUDIBLE MALE GAZE
AND MALE ARBITERS OF TASTE

Music made by women for the most part is being curated through male tastemakers and gatekeepers. How does this affect the music being recorded and produced? Are artists and projects held back by this? If so, who's held back and in what ways? Is it a case of label pushback? What are your experiences?

Abhita Austin: Well, I think there's just less of us. I think, from what I've experienced, women producers—in relation to how male gatekeepers affect that—we are a lot of times looked over or not considered, and I am guessing that's the case because there's just not a lot of us there. I remember when I started interning years ago, and I went to Bad Boy [Records] first, and they were not accepting interns. And then I went to Quad Recording Studios, and they took me on, but I remember the management was all male. And I was being pushed, although I was studying music technology and audio engineering at New York University—they knew that; I was one of the only people who [was] studying, you know, back in the day. This was like the late '90s; there were not a lot of schools for audio engineering. So they knew I was studying, and I was slowly being steered toward management and toward the front desk, and it made me think, "I have to put myself forward and make it known that this is what I am interested in."

I think in relation to women music producers and male gatekeepers, there is just a lack of sensitivity, or there's just a certain gaze, and they just don't see women in certain roles. They just might assume, from my experience, that, "Why would you wanna?"—even though you're saying [you want to]. I have had male gatekeepers tell me that I'm not an engineer. . . . So I guess, to come back to the question we are talking about, I think it kind of allows for less women producers to come through the pipeline. I have had male gatekeepers tell me that I am not an engineer or that I'm not, like, the caliber to be an engineer—which in hindsight is crazy.

Because I work independently, none of the projects I am working on are running through that channel. It's also a different time; it's a totally different time. Music has greatly been democratized because of the Internet.

So, as far as pushback, it's not overt in a sense because the men that I am dealing with, they understand what it is intellectually—and some of them more than others—but, like, there is a sense of not taking women producers seriously unless there's a persona that they can grab on to. This is not in all cases; there are a couple of cases where they respect the music. But lots of times in choosing the women that they want to bring into the fold, it's a visual more so than the music.

I am even thinking about artists because, you know, I come from a lot of hip-hop music, a lot of R & B music, and even a lot of the women that are considered feminist in those categories are ridiculously misogynistic—just ridiculously violent toward women. And I'm not talking about physical violence; it's mental. It's affecting how other younger women envision themselves, and so that's always fascinating in an unfortunate way, and that happens a lot.

Leslie M. G. Bird: I don't actually have any experience with the music-recording artists. I'm on the technical side. I am not a music-recording engineer. I do audio for film, radio, and television and just teach recording arts. So my role is more of an engineer, not a producer. I see what happens to my students when they go that route, and I see that a lot of women are discouraged from working behind the glass. That's the angle I come at it.

Hillary Johnson: I think it really only—in my experience—really only affects female singers, like solo artists, in the sense that, if they are working with a male producer, just from what women have told me over the years, is that . . . they don't necessarily feel comfortable. They feel sometimes that the producers are working them too hard for reasons other than the art. [Laughs] Just to sort of push them around sort of thing. But that, you know, has been such a long time since I have really heard anyone tell me that sort of story. It's probably been twenty years, so maybe it's different now.

I think that there's enough political correctness that's been going on for long enough, at least, that it shouldn't really matter whether the producer is a man or woman or that the artist is a man or a woman. I would think that it's better than, say, twenty to twenty-five years ago, but it could just be wishful thinking. Most of the stuff that I've worked has not been in the pop-culture realm, so my only experience with that is seeing it in the pop world, where records have to be more than just the music, more than just the song; it has to be the whole product—the person as the product, the band as the product. So I've never really personally experienced that. I've only been—I keep myself at a different level of things so that I don't have to even think about that stuff for that reason. That doesn't interest me. I am here to make records. I am not here to do business, I guess.

Sylvia Massy: Oh, wow—good question. I have just done a big research project on who's managing the big bands these days. It's actually about fifty-fifty men and women on the managers who are doing these big projects and working with big artists. So I can't say that it's entirely men in my experience with A&R [artists and repertoire] people, and with labels, I don't think they are as much the tastemakers as they were in the past. But the A&R people are about fifty-fifty men and women. I think that even in the higher-ups at the labels, there's a lot of women in management and in administration. Maybe there's less in the actual decision making of who's putting money into what. But honestly, I might have a different perspective than most women on the differences between men and women in the music industry. As far as I'm concerned, the women that are in the management and labels, that's as much opportunity there as there is.

However, in the recording studios and production, there is a difference—way more men than women. But I also think that that's not due to discrimination in the workplace. I think it's more about women's choices on what they want to do with their lives. Because working in the entertainment industry and the technical side of the industry is a very demanding career, and so, you know, when you are producing a project, you basically have to join that group. Let's say it's a band; you're like the new member, basically, for the length of time recording, and you really live and breathe that project, and it often takes fourteen-hour days to get through that project, and that kind of pushes away all your social time and family time that would typically be, you know, what a woman would want to have more of.

I think women generally gravitate toward more of the parts of the music industry that allow them more time, and that would be A&R, journalism, and those kinds of things, and I imagine it allows them more time for social life that women really like. In my case, for some reason, I really love being in the studio so much that I pretty much just kind of pushed away the whole social world and pushed away the whole family idea and just really concentrated on my career in music production. So I am an odd bird, as far as that goes, I think. I gave a long-winded explanation—probably way more than you needed. So the original question, "How does it affect the choices for music?" and . . . I think that women have good taste in music, as well as men. I think that perhaps you're going to get more scantily clad women onstage just because that sells better. It sells better for both men and women. I think that women also like to see someone who's an ideal onstage, so we might want to see someone who's in really good shape and can really dance and is a beautiful person. But there's also those that aren't necessarily the beauty queens out there—these days more so than ever. It's more a reflection on society to have, let's say, Meghan Trainor or Adele, you know, who does not have the ideal body, and so maybe these are the new ideals. And so, I guess, I still think that the choice of music is a reflection on the society today.

Johnette Napolitano: I think the first thing we'd have to do is define *producer*. What exactly is that role or job description?

Kerry Pompeo: Well, I think about it being less of an issue now, but I think, just going back to when there were Britney Spears and there were . . . the overly-sexualized-women kind of image, a lot of that happened. But at the same time there were also so many great female bands—like all-female bands. Like L7—they were the total opposite of what that was, and to be honest, I don't know if they had female producers.

   Kallie Marie: They didn't.

Kerry Pompeo: It's a real kind of power play, as well, because, to your question, the tables were turned because for a long time women were, you know, . . . "Make sure she can dance while she's singing that," or, you know, "Make sure she's singing about something that little girls want to run out and buy," or, you know, "Throw on a skirt . . ." I do think times are changing on that. I really haven't had any personal experiences where producers had to be like, "Oh, like let's sex it up," or anything like that. So, no pushback, and I haven't experienced that personally as an engineer.

Ebonie Smith: Okay, so, with tastemakers traditionally being men and gatekeepers—I would say that can have a tremendous effect on the music because I think there's a very specific perspective that starts before you get in the room that influences who gets in the room. Right, so, if there are preconceived notions about what men bring to the table versus what women bring to the table that are purely based on assumption, then I think folks in the room who a lot of times think alike, right, which is not a problem as long as there is balance somewhere that helps to counteract. Because people typically like to make music with folks that they like to hang around. If the guys have their specific environments and enjoy making music about certain things that are culturally a part of their environments, then obviously that carries onto the production process because the gatekeepers are primarily male. So, yeah, I think, when thinking of specific gatekeepers, we are talking obviously about A&R executives, we're talking about publishers, we are talking about managers, and, to some extent, lawyers—entertainment lawyers who help broker these deals and help to facilitate relationships between artists and engineers, as well as studios. So if you have a large majority of men in these positions, then it creates a very specific perspective that persists even during the "just getting to know one another" because so much of music is relationship building; music making is relationship building and hanging out outside of the studio. So where these guys will be finding peers has just as much influence over how they find colleagues and people they want to work with. I think that's what ultimately, specifically what . . . we are talking about—the A&R executives, even major label heads, and publishers, managers. . . . It's going to most certainly influence the culture of the studio, for sure.

What I've been probably the most frustrated about is relationship building in ways that give me opportunities to move around and work with different types of people. It's rare that I will find someone who I could work with who will say, "Right, well, why don't you come over here and work with me on this other project?" There's always the barrier when it comes to building deeper relationships with male gatekeepers. I don't see it as much with female artists; there's always the desire to follow up and continue working together after the initial interaction because our perspectives are similar. If you want, like—and I said this before—people want to make music with folks they have something in common with and who seem to understand where they're coming from, and that's, . . . I would say, 90 percent of productive studio session is common ground. With the women artists as the producer and as the engineer, there is more of a willingness to follow up after the initial interaction to work together again. And I don't see that with the men as often, and it's not because we didn't have a productive session; it's maybe just because they don't hang out with me, and that's 90 percent of how you get business. People have to want to hang out, and they have to wanna be friends with you. If there's the feeling that you are just boring, in terms of your perspective and sometimes that otherness of being a woman, is just enough to keep you from getting invited to the next thing. Not that you're not a great engineer, not that you're not competent. It's just, can we be, "Do I want to get a beer with you? Do I want to talk about random things that guys like to talk about?" You know? So that's what I've noticed. I've worked with women all over the world who I still keep in contact with because we really enjoy each other as friends and we have similar perspectives, and it always makes its way into the music and art.

Andrea Yankovsky: In my personal experience is one thing, in my opinion; in terms [of] historical opinion, I would say that, looking over time, of especially popular music, of giving a male-oriented, often-sexist view of women in popular songs and lyrics and things like that. In terms of my own personal experience, I really got going right when Napster hit. So when you look at my age, I think I was reading something in the *Huffington Post* very recently about the people who are in between the generation of—what do they call it now, the Xennials, now—you got your first email account in college. So I fall within that, so I would say that there was already a certain amount of transition in the industry, driven by people, by the public, and so when I entered the industry and was really immersed in it, people were still working in the studios; there [was] still a certain amount of gatekeeping, but it was changing. So I think a lot of the bigger, older projects, there's definitely more of a gendered perspective. But there was the whole undercurrent of an upwelling of sort of new artists, new perspectives, and there were more choices for females.

I wasn't involved so much with labels at that point or A&R. I think a lot of the times, it was an issue of who is the producer, and the producer at that point really was the keeper of how they were going to deal with the label and how they were going to move the project forward.

Anonymous: Women and men hear differently and have different experiences with the world around them. So at the most basic level, having mostly men curate all music really narrows the range of ideas and musical possibilities that the public can be exposed to. If a woman's idea is not digestible for the men around her, she may have a harder time breaking through the noise and receiving support unless she has power or wealth on her own. By imposing a male filter on women's artistic visions, we lose their raw authenticity and end up with a watered-down version of the female experience—like we hear in most current mainstream music.

From what I've seen, there are a lot of male producers who specifically seek out talented or interesting women to produce—I believe in many ways because they think an attractive woman will be more marketable than they are, and so they can use the woman as a vessel for their creative ideas or live vicariously, or through royalties, through their success. I also think there's an assumption that there must be a man behind every woman's production. I think some male producers have a fantasy of "discovering" a new talent or being the savior, the enabler, the wizard behind the curtain of a female artist.

times it appears like a producer will make changes to a song/ just for the sake of making changes—to put his stamp on the music and to ensure that he has some ownership in the material. I'm sure this could happen with both male and female artists, but I've witnessed female artists struggle with this more. Unfortunately, some of these changes don't necessarily always help the music, leaving many female artists frustrated and potentially losing interest in the project and giving up.

What ways can having women — men, too — as producers help subvert the music industry, specifically with regard to tastemakers taking risks on female artists that don't fit the traditional molds — for example, artists that don't fit the "sexy diva" or "heartbroken siren" mold?

Abhita Austin: I would say that you could subvert that by starting your own projects and being entrepreneurial. Understanding that when you become an engineer—and I did not know that when I started— that means that I am an entrepreneur. I did not realize that you have to sell yourself. You have to be looking for artists. When you start, you're just trying to learn. I realized, when I was interning, that the people who [were] winning and staying, they were entrepreneurial; they were bringing in artists. They were connecting with artists. You have to. That's the only way.

Hillary Johnson: Well, I think that men and women who have worked in the studio have had bad experiences in general, and because the majority of producers and engineers are male, that just means that they are having bad experiences with men. I think that I've had plenty of experiences where I worked with men, and I've worked with women, and they've all told me, "Wow, it's like a breath of fresh air, working with you." A lot of them attribute that to me being a woman and just being more, I dunno, open to them trying new things. Maybe it's a male vocalist who normally sings deep and wants to try falsetto but hasn't been comfortable before because of whatever reason. Or it's women who, even they shouldn't have to feel any different—most male producers are very professional and are just there to get the job done; they're there to get a good record, get a good performance—but I know that there are women who feel more comfortable with females in the studio. So I think that there's definitely people that are broken, that are out there making records that have had experiences that have changed after working with a person of another gender.

Sylvia Massy: Wow. Well, when I work with a musical artist—and I am working with one right now; her name is Angelina, and she has limited knowledge of songwriting; she has some songs in her head but no experience recording or using any of the recording equipment—so my thought to help her and help other women, if possible, is to give them the keys, basically. We sat down with her and showed her how to use the equipment: "Here's how you record; you set up a track here; this is how you set up a microphone; these are the good microphones to use for your voice. This is how you run a session; here's how you hire players; and here's the flow of an arrangement." I spent a good amount of time with her to give her the skills to be able to produce her own music. I think that is a big thing that women who have experience with production can help the artist to gain control over what they're doing. Then you get the real thing—you're getting women who are writing the music as well as recording and producing their own music, and I think that's fantastic.

There's not that many out there. I'd have to say, not with the recording side of it, but Lady Gaga is just—I admire this person so much because she writes and she plays. She knows how to play these instruments, you know? She's a fantastic writer. Meghan Trainor, again, is someone who started very young writing music, and that's how she got her opportunities because she was just writing great songs and bringing them to other artists. And then I believe the story is that Elle Reede said, "Why don't we have you sing this? Here's this great song; why don't you sing it?" Taylor Swift is another person who's writing songs, who plays, who sings. You know, I don't know how much she's involved in the production, but I think that today, more than ever, the women are gaining control over the production of their music. So we can all help each other by learning how to produce, how to use the equipment, so we don't have to depend on the men to do it. Unless we need them for something else. They could go get coffee!

Johnette Napolitano: I have to be honest and say that this conversation in the first place is rather dated. Great producers have been gay men in the closet. Gay male record executives. Easily, I know as many male musicians who have been sexually propositioned if not assaulted as women. Artists don't really get a lot of respect, period, male or female. For example, even as an artist, if I co-produce with a "producer," they get paid from the record, but I don't. The male/female nonissue is irrelevant in a rock genre with a White, androgynous face. The real issue is artist respect and the place in the food chain, not male/female.

Kerry Pompeo: Well, I think that now more than ever there is the ability to not have to conform and be part of the major [labels]. So I think that has allowed people to just be themselves. Whether they are a sexy siren or whether they're a screaming punk-rock maniac or whether they are just kind of, like, sad but not like that overly kind of sad, typically kind of, like, woman-y thing. More than ever, that's just the climate. We can access fans for any niche. That's kind of broken down walls, and the independent record label has come back, so less and less you are having to fit the mold of what large companies are asking for. More than ever, we are able to kind of put a middle finger up and be like, "No. We wanna do—this is what we like, we like what we're doing, and what we are doing, we're doing it on our terms."

Ebonie Smith: You know, I really think it starts with women: Women have to be more supportive of other women. For the one or two women in positions of influence that are sprinkled around various industries, they have to be secure enough in themselves to bring up to . . . I really believe that if each one in our industries brought up another ten, we would be in really good shape. So I think it's about women creating collectives around each other—and not just create collectives but realizing what we have in collective organizing is power and strength and finding ways to commercialize that. Because that's when the industry as a whole takes notice. Does it make money, you know? This is a music business; it's not just enough to be like, "Oh, yeah, we're girls. We're over here making great art!" Like, is it good? Does anybody care? I think people do care, and I think it is good, but I think the onus is on women to support one another and to really make up our minds about whether or not we want to see true diversity. Because some of the bigger power players in the business are women; it's not a lot of them, but it's enough of them to really make an impact if they strategically decide to help other women out. And let me just clarify one thing: I said it starts with women. Okay, so I'm not saying that we don't have other societal issues. Everybody needs to do a little work, and I think it's started. It's gonna happen, but it's gonna have to start with women to see the changes we wanna see.

Andrea Yankovsky: Oh, it's huge. Absolutely huge, especially as women develop more community and start to work with each other as opposed to work against each other. There's less scarcity now; we are not chasing crumbs anymore. So from the perspective of when there's scarce resources and people have to compete for them, a lot of times women were other women's worst enemies. But now there's more, I think the mentality has changed, too, in terms of people really collaborating and working together and helping push each other forward and realizing women now have their own "old boys'" network, and it's a big deal. But at the same time, I think, it started working in the '90s; there was the whole Lilith Fair thing. There was a lot of, like—I hate to call it, but people called it *girl power*, which is just completely . . . [Laughs] But they were young women, right? And you wouldn't have called it *boy power*, right? [Laughs] These were women, and they were pushing for—and they were calling things out, like, who was it, what was her name . . . her lyrics were like, "I'm a bitch / I'm a lover, / I'm a sinner / and a saint," you know, and "I will not be ashamed." And you would get that, and people coming up were Shawn Colvin, Paula Cole, that whole movement and at the same time sort of early influences and other things that I feel like, in a lot of ways—early on there was this feeling that, if you were really pushing things forward and really had a feminist perspective—or even just a profemale perspective—you often got labeled as a lesbian or a dyke. There's nothing wrong with being a lesbian, but I think that label was just immediately applied, and it sucks. And at the same [time] it is also so true that we really are indebted to people like k.d. lang, Melissa Etheridge, the Indigo Girls—all those people that were really trying to put positive messages [out] for women. It wasn't so much like it was different from the earlier iterations of the women's movement. It was more subtle. I think people were starting to ask questions of, "Can women have it all?" You're making choices between career and family and just basically being able to have some sort of a life-work balance. That's that term—I'd be curious to see when that term really started coming about. Like, life-work balance.

I think another thing about that, too, also—you had permission to be female—in that a lot of the times, in male-dominated industries, you basically had to become a man. I see it in other industries, as well, to the extent in my industry where they are not even able to dress like a woman.

Anonymous: Of course the more diverse the tastemakers and producers are, the more diverse art and ideas we'll see. I think that by having more female producers in the industry, proving that women are competent at it, people in general will start to trust women more in that role, and we'll see more varied artistry and people taking greater risks. Hopefully we will also hear less stories about women feeling trapped in a situation or having a career crushed after navigating the sexual advances of a producer, manager, et cetera, that they're working with. More women in media production leads to greater cultural democracy, more opportunities to break barriers of communication between men and women, and unlimited and untapped potential of humanity's growth.

There are some perceived and internalized gendered views of what women "should sound like" based on what male tastemakers find acceptable, suitable, and/or attractive. How do you think having more women in the music industry, both as producers and label heads, will affect this?

Kerry Pompeo: I think it's just beneficial because—I don't know how often other people are reading the liner notes, but when I was coming up, I always was reading the liner notes, and I think it's a really nice to see more and more women's names in those things, and I think it just inspirational. And it's not even so much like shouting out inspiration; but it's like this subliminal fact that they can read these lines, and it's not just all men's names. So I think that's very important—that it doesn't even have to be so in-your-face but just that it's there and that, you know, if the presence is there, it is major.

Ebonie Smith: I think the age-old concept is "Sex sells," and that is completely true. But I think there are lots of different perspectives on what is sexy and can be sexy and how sexiness is perceived. And for women, I think, provide more interesting perspectives on what it means to be a woman—in art. There are about a thousand ways to do that and to be convincing and not just be convincing but to be relatable to lots of audiences. And I think you are seeing it now with artists like Young MA, who is masculine-presenting and identifies as gay and lesbian. You're seeing all these different perspectives on what it means to be relatable and what it means to be attractive and what it means to be sexy even. You're seeing so many different perspectives on that as women are taking full control of their brands—and not just from the perspective of artists but who they are choosing to collaborate with, from the branding perspective, from production perspective to promotion perspective, PR perspective. We are seeing alternative definitions of femininity, which I think is something that is being driven by women feeling confident enough to assert themselves in the industry. I don't think that is coming from traditional school of thought of what's sexy, what sells, and what type of women artists can make it. Now, you still have the pervasive concept that women have to be sexy and oversexualized, but you are seeing that counterbalanced by strong women who are saying, "No—I can do this the way I feel comfortable and still make a dent commercially and culturally," like Janelle Monáe, you know? Even Katy Perry. And obviously Alicia Keys has been a huge proponent of women being comfortable in their own skin and taking off their makeup. So I do think that more women just be feeling confident enough to assert their vision for their brand is helping a lot.

Anonymous: Diversity leads to more diversity, so of course adding any diversity to an industry will create a change in what is deemed normal or appropriate. With more women making decisions, I think women's raw talent will shine through without a layer of sexual interest attached. But I don't think women will necessarily look/sound differently right away because women have been conditioned their whole lives to admire and recycle the images of attractive women that have been fed to them by the advertising industry. However, a woman showcasing her sexuality in the way she wants—versus what was developed as a team of men working behind the scenes—will create art that is more real, nuanced, and complex.

PARADIGM SHIFTS IN THE MUSIC INDUSTRY
What part have the paradigm shifts in the music industry played in paving the way for more female producers? How will similar problems continue to occur but through different channels — as in heads of streaming services, media, et cetera?

Hillary Johnson: Maybe? I mean, because of the fact that there's so much music being produced on computers, and computers are something that women are taught, just like men, in school, so maybe women are just more comfortable with a computer, and they only have to learn about microphones and music and that sort of thing rather than . . . a lot less technical stuff. So maybe because we are taught to not be technical, maybe it's just easier for women to start something and to continue it because there's less technical challenges.

Johnette Napolitano: Once again, I'm not sure everyone understands exactly what the job is. I don't [think] there's any easy way to get anywhere around the usual channels: sacrifice, work, apprentice. And there shouldn't be.

Kerry Pompeo: Well, I will tell you, in my experience, I've been do-ing this, like, about fifteen years, and I've seen a shift even in my own career where people used to have to come to me or come to a studio in order to do what they need to get done, done. Nowadays—and my career evolved around this—but technology went or was released from being only in the grips of the people who had the money, the very small percentage that had the money basically to run a studio, to it being very like a democracy, where anybody can afford it and do it in their own bedroom! And not be scared! You can go and be whomever you want to be and record, make a decent-sounding recording behind your four walls and in your comfort zone. So because the technology became ac-cessible—more accessible—to anyone, behind their own comfort zone and closed doors. I think where people would have been a little bit more shy to step into a male-dominated room, they could learn for themselves at their own pace and explore in a comfortable way. So I think that that shift in the business—and that's, like, what happened a lot to my career. People used to have to come to me to record everything. Then I was getting a lot of just mixing jobs because it was like, "Hey, I recorded this at home; can you make this? Can you use your ear to make this sound better and nicer?" Now I'm seeing more female producers and stuff coming back to the studio because they have that foundation, and they've been accustomed to it. So the studio, as a business, is becoming more of "Let's get back in the studio and create." Where for a while it was like, "Here's the stuff from home . . ." But I think that that really kind of helped; the shift in the business of recording music really helped with democratizing who had the ability to do so.

Ebonie Smith: Obviously technology. I gotta harp on that because the ease [with] which you can make music on a laptop and really have a product that sounds so great and in some cases radio-ready—that's changed . . . the landscape a lot. Social media has changed the land-scape a lot; the ease with which you can disseminate and distribute your music via distribution platforms and social networks is amazing. And lastly, I think you've seen a growth of educational institutions with music-production programs, which is really wonderful because it creates a legitimate means for women to be in safe environments and learn and to receive credentials and opportunities to do studio internships—opportunities that wouldn't ordinarily be there without the infrastructure of [a] major university or a college, getting girls in doors they would ordinarily just have to network their way in through networks that they don't really have access to or know exist. So when you are coming through a school, you really kind of skip the aspect of just having to know certain people or certain networks, certain blogs, or whatever. So I think those were probably the three main things, I would say: social media, advances in technology, and school programs.

Andrea Yankovsky: I think it has opened up a lot, but at the same time, it also takes more to stand out. The doors are opened in terms of you don't have to rely on someone giving you a shot. You know, production's much more entrepreneurial now, and again I feel like, as women get together and learn about how they do business, how they want to do business, how they can do business, that makes a huge difference. At the same time, it depends on who their market is, a lot of the time. Because at the end of the day, we are in the music business, right? So at the end of the day, we are selling something; we are selling music. And when you talk about: Who are we selling to? What are they going to buy? And there's so many factors in that, but we like to think that we are making music, we are putting it out there, and we hope someone wants it. But there are a lot of people out there . . . who are looking at it as more of a business strategy and saying, "This is the market; let's develop the music that they want." So it's varied—very variable. Up at the top, it takes longer to change unless there's a consciousness that's driving it. A lot of the times, when you are at the top, why mess with what's working? You don't have an impetus to change unless it's something that's really important to you. So you have a lot of men at the top; why would they change unless they care? And when you get women up at the top, that kind of depends on the individual person.

Anonymous: Because it's more accessible, anyone with a computer and Internet connection can record, produce, and release music. Women can produce themselves and don't need to wait to be signed to a label or "discovered" by another producer. However, there are still barriers to entry; like, a learning curve of recording/mixing and having the time to do it all and support oneself is challenging. But there is less of a reliance on men for the technical aspects than there was before.

As long as the executives are all male, women will not be democratically represented. I remember a couple years ago when Apple Music head and key music industry influencer Jimmy Iovine said women need help finding music to listen to when they sit around with their girlfriends complaining about boys. Women are huge music consumers and concert-ticket buyers, but there's still this idea that we don't understand music in a way that men do. That really showed how far we still have to go in being seen as equals.

There was also a recent study which found that women and people of color who help each other end up getting worse performance reviews from their superiors than those who did not. So often they end up not trying to help their demographic in their workplace because it ends up punishing them. So until women represent at least half of the positions in power, the male taste will always rule.

"CHICK MUSIC" AND THE ASSUMED "FEMININE TOUCH"

If it is made more known that a record is produced by a woman, especially if the artist is also a woman, is the music at risk of being deemed "feminine" — for example, in the way that visual art made by women is often treated or termed "women's art," or what I like to call the *chick-flick effect* as it happens with film? Have you had any experiences of this? Are we at risk of this occurring as we start to have more women producers? How do we prevent this from occurring?

Sylvia Massy: No, because I choose music that is really hard, and I really love hard music. Tool? That's not feminine. Or Slayer or System of a Down. I love aggressive music. I don't think that I soften it in any way. However, once I worked with the band Sublime, and I created a bunch of backing vocals, which may have been a little too soft for them, and I got some eye-rolling. And it was like, "Okay, okay, okay—I get it." But that's about it. I generally work with aggressive bands, but then I don't limit myself, either. As a woman, I have experiences with all types of music. So I do zydeco, I do country, I worked with Johnny Cash, and I do straight-edge pop rock. I did Tom Petty and the Heartbreakers and Chili Peppers, and I worked with Prince for three years, too, so I try to have a well-rounded discography. But I'm good with hard music, and I think the way that I gain the trust of an artist—because, you know, a hard band, they're usually covered with tattoos, nose rings comin' outta their face everywhere, horrible hair, whatever. If I walk into the session and I start cursin' and throwin' stuff, you know, right away, they're like, "Okay, okay, okay, we'll do whatever you say, lady." So I establish myself just by throwing my weight around right away.

> **Kallie Marie:** Okay, so I guess from the get-go, you have always worked with hard music, so no one was ever going to be concerned that that was an issue?

Sylvia Massy: Right! And maybe that's the best thing I could have done, was to start with hard music so I don't get pigeonholed into, "Oh, she just does girl music." I have never had that problem, ever.

Johnette Napolitano: This business amuses me in their self-importance. The punters don't care who produced a record. I'm not sure millions of kids know who produced Ariana Grande and don't care. But let me tell you, I had no idea who that girl was and saw her walk through LAX, and she *owned* that airport, and you can bet she knows her power.

Kerry Pompeo: Well, in my experience, I've never had at least anybody outwardly say that to me. But me, I've had that held under my, you know, that stigma kind of, kind of as a bar for me to kind of overcome. I think that was always, you know—as females, we have to try harder, at least when we are breaking in, and that was always something that I held over myself. Like, I didn't want someone to hear it and think that [Whispers] that it sounded like chick music. That was a bar that I set for myself; nobody else set it for me or told me, but that was just something that I did. So maybe where I see the risk—and this is where I sometimes have struggles, and I totally appreciate it; I'm not knocking, like, the women's groups that are meant to give us a place to vent and bond and empower, and come into a collective, but I feel like there is a—like, we do detriment to ourselves if it has to be, like, a female thing because then we're putting ourselves in a box that is going to make it very easy for people to say it's *that*. I think that it's not a realistic depiction of the world, too, because, you know, it's not 100 percent men; it's not 100 percent women. So I think that when it does go, you know, the Lilith Fair route, that you really don't give people a choice but to say, "It's Lilith Fair," or say, "It's a chick group," or say, "It's chick rock." Because at that point, they're not lying. It is chicks; they are playing rock music or chick hip-hop; they're not lying if it's an all-female group. But this stereotype, even they might be, like, have more balls than any dude. The stereotype might follow them because it's all women, and that is something that needs to be broken down because what is "chick" and what is "girly"?

Kallie Marie: Yeah, because we don't have that stereotype every time we have a band that's all guys. It's not suddenly—

Kerry Pompeo: —Yeah, it's not a "dude band."

Kallie Marie: We don't call it "dude rock." Therein lies the problem: the perception is that anything that men do is for everyone and anything that women do, especially if it's all female, then it—

Kerry Pompeo: —is "Just for Girls."

Kallie Marie: Right. And that's what I am calling the "chick-flick effect," which we see in film. Do we run the risk of that occurring in music when we start having more female producers?

Kerry Pompeo: That's interesting. You know, I am working with a London vocalist, and she specifically said to me, "You know, I'm writing music because I want, like, the dudes listening on the subway to not be embarrassed that he's listening to my music," you know? So it was very much so—when we are writing and creating the music—again setting that bar, the self-aware bar for ourselves—that we don't want it to be "chick rock." I think that has been set by the record companies . . . that kind of made it that way. I don't think chicks, like, we are not flying this flag, like, "Let's make it really soft and dreamy," you know, and, like, "We are crying because our boyfriends broke up with us." I think that because the paradigm of the industry has changed that this is less of that "chick rock," it has less potential because we didn't create "chick rock." So when we make our recipe that is only inclusive of women, I think it has the tendency to be categorized "chick rock." But I think what that is, is changing.

I think it's a very important thing; it doesn't need to be shouted, like, "Hey, we are all girls!" I think that that's another, like, kind of detriment that we do by having to feel like we have to announce it; then it's calling attention to the fact that we are chicks, and we don't want that. We just want to be engineers; we want to be producers; we want to be artists. We don't want to be, like, chick, boy, girl, Black, White, anything, you know, like, labels especially. What we do is art; what I do is technical, but it's a technical art. There's no labels in art, and there shouldn't be. And I think people put them there. And sometimes it is the people that are creating it that are putting it there and just have enough confidence that they don't need that label to say that "I'm a chick and doing it." You know just, like, "I'm doing it."

Ebonie Smith: I don't know that I am too much opposed to the "chick flick" concept, in film. "Chick flicks" make money, and "chick flicks" also bring out people to the movies—lots of women, lots of mothers, lots of grandmothers—because they come out because they want to see "chick flicks." I think the term is pejorative, but I don't think it is necessarily a problem. The parallel that I see in music is obviously "women's anthems." You know, I would like to see more women like Missy Elliott making timeless women anthems. I don't care if women get pushed into that category "Oh, she makes woman anthems." I mean, if they are great records that make money, that inspire generations, and create songs like "Lady Marmalade" and "Survivor" and whatever else, you know, I'm not necessarily opposed to whatever society wants to call what women do well. The problem that would make me most concerned is if women aren't getting paid what the guys are getting paid and if women are not getting the regular opportunities to stretch their wings outside of certain styles and genres of music.

Kallie Marie: That was my concern.

Ebonie Smith: That would mean that's the thing we have to be concerned about. And I think if the doors are open properly for women in the studio to do their best work, and if they deliver, then I don't think it will be a problem. If they want to call us whatever—like, call us whatever or label our music as whatever—it doesn't matter, as long as they just pay us. Like, that's kind of the thing that I am most concerned about. I am not really concerned about the stereotypes in the way of it.

Andrea Yankovsky: I think that effect is probably more prevalent when the artist is a woman. But so many times, I don't know how much people actually pay attention to who the producer is, unless a big deal has been made about it. It was funny because I remember when people would ask me what music did I like; this was back before Pandora or Spotify would say, "Here are some recommendations." And I would say, "If you find a piece of music that you like, don't just stop at the artist; find out who produced it!" That's such a revelation to non-music people, people that aren't in the industry. I would make that recommendation to people. That was eye-opening to them, and their musical taste would expand. So I don't have a good feel for how much people are actually looking at producers.

Anonymous: Yes, there is definitely almost a stigma around dominantly female projects. Not necessarily that it's always "feminine" because I think women have found a place in rock, for example, that can be gritty. But men are so used to being the center of attention in films and albums that when something is not centered around men, they think that it's not for them. They don't realize that most of the media we consume does not center around us, yet we don't differentiate and ignore it.

A very common issue is that often art/music made by women gets treated like it's its own genre. We see this in lineups for festival bills, when there is a specific, limited number of openings for "female" bands . . . but there is never a limit for the number of "male" bands. I think having more women producers will hopefully reduce this issue. The more diverse content created by women that goes out there, the less people can lump it into a category or treat it as all the same. It's also important to chronicle the work done by women, as historically it has been erased, undocumented, or forgotten. I've come across albums produced by women forty years ago, and I can barely find any information about the producers. Yet, I can easily find info about the one guy who played trumpet on one track. As Björk said, show pictures of women behind desks doing the grunt work. Show people that women are doing it, and they can no longer deny it.

Can you think of any situations where it was assumed you couldn't do or produce a certain style of music solely because of your gender? Something like, "Oh, we can't have her produce it; we need a hard, aggressive, heavy sound. We want to make a tough record." If so, what were your tactics for handling this? How did it influence your production of the recording, both negatively and positively?

Abhita Austin: [Laughs] I have, and it's funny to me because it always comes from—it's usually men. Because we work with, in this field, majority men, and I am sure it's the same for you. Like, the majority of even artists that come into the studio are men, and that's interesting because outside of that, I know of a lot of women artists. But for some reason, I guess there is a deficit between women artists, and there are more male artists. It's really strange! Like, when I think about it, even when I was in a commercial studio or even in my own studio, the majority of people coming in are men.

Hillary Johnson: I've never been personally not asked to do a record—at least that I know of—or told, "Well maybe that's not the right thing for you." Because, I dunno, I started off doing hard-core. I started out doing punk, and the only thing that I've never really gotten the opportunity to do is pop stuff, but that's also because I started off in kind of an independent world and kind of stayed there and liked it, and I didn't really reach out for anything different. So I don't know if it's just because there's not enough women that are known that do pop and rock and hip-hop. Maybe if anyone is out there experiencing the fact that they're not able to get a gig because of the fact that they are a woman, is maybe it's because of the fact that they just don't have experience and they think that it's because they are a woman. I don't know . . .

Sylvia Massy: Not because I'm a woman. But I do have limitations on the sound of the music that I am able to produce only because I believe that there's different types of music and different types of producers. The different types would be the engineer-type producer, which is where I started because I knew how to use the recording equipment. So when I would work with an artist, I would say, "Here—try this, try that," and we would work together, and I would manipulate the recording equipment to do my productions. Then there's the other type of producer, which is the musician producer, and that person generally writes a lot of the music. I think Pharrell Williams started there. He was producing artists by basically writing the song and finding the artist to play the song or sing the song. I'm not that type of producer, for the most part. I'll do arrangements—like whole arrangements, string arrangements—but I don't play the instruments. So I'm not a musician-producer. Then the third type of producer is the fan producer, someone who doesn't touch the equipment or play any instruments but just knows good music. Like Rick Rubin—he's that kind of producer. So if there's any limitation that I have, it's not necessarily because I'm a woman, but it is that I am not a programmer, so I am not going to be able to write the songs. Generally, I don't write the songs that the artists play. So that's probably what I would not be hired for—if there's anything that has to do with programming the music.

Johnette Napolitano: Never. If anything, I remember laying down a temporary drum track for someone once, and they were taken aback by my time. It's because singers are treated as the vain divas—male *or* female. Most of the time they are.

Kerry Pompeo: Not to my face; maybe behind my back? Maybe there were talks behind my back when I was out on break or while I had my headphones on or while I was out with the artist. Again, I'm going back to setting the bar for ourselves: I think I was aware that that could be a problem, so I always backed it up with really good work. So even if they said that, that was dissolved by the first take. That was always my MO, I knew, and especially when I started doing this in the early 2000s. It was so different than it is now. And so I always made it—I was aware that it could be harder or I could be judged, so I just made sure that I had tricks up my sleeve. When you make people feel comfortable, they're not going to question your gender or even think about it or make it an issue if they know they are in good hands, and that's really [what] any artist or anybody who you're creating with, at the end of the day, should want.

Again, there's still people that don't want to work with a girl, but at the end of the day, that's their problem, and I think those people are dying out.

Ebonie Smith: No, I can't. Just because I don't have any hard evidence that that was what was coming, you know, that that's what the reason was. It could have been coming from because I was Black or could have been because I was young. I've been underestimated—sure, plenty of times and not just in music. But I never really—you know, the thing about it is, you never really kind of know unless somebody comes out and tells you, "I don't think you can do this because you're a woman." You never really know that that's why. So I can't really think of an instance where anybody's ever done that.

Andrea Yankovsky: Not style of music, per se. I think that was also the time that I was working in because we did have people who paved the way. I would say the inference that I would make from that would, is, say, "Can women work on edgy, hard-core music?" And women had already started paving the way for that.

Anonymous: I haven't had that exact experience, but I have seen a lot of men apologize for swearing, start acting differently, or think they have to be more proper because they're around a woman. I worked with a touring engineer once who apologized and said he was nervous around women while we were discussing the input list. So sometimes you can visibly see the confusion and cognitive dissonance on their face when they realize there's a "girl" doing a "man's" job. It's exhausting, but it's also fun to see your mere existence chipping away at these tired stereotypes. For the most part, I try to be friendly but firm with people, do the best job I can, and let my work speak for itself.

TRADITIONAL STUDIO HIERARCHY: WHEN IS THERE MORE THAN ONE WOMAN?

How is the experience of the traditional studio hierarchy between engineer/ producer, tape op, intern, et cetera, different for women when the team is predominantly female, in your experience? How was this received by clients who were not anticipating a woman or a team of more than one woman? If you have not had this opportunity, how do you think it has impacted you to not have had the chance to have other women in your workplace?

Abhita Austin: I don't know how much difference it was because there was only one, who was above me, and then there was one, she came in after me; she was coming in as I was becoming an assistant. To me, psychologically, it was nice to see another woman. I felt like I did not receive any mentorship or help from the one above me, for sure. But it was good. I can't discredit having not seen them. It meant something to see other women. How much help that was to my psyche, subliminally or subconsciously, I felt like—for the intern below me, I think I was friendly. I was again, too, I was an assistant. I felt like I had no—like, I did not have a lot of power. In that whole hierarchy. I was trying to make my way myself. So I think other than just like camaraderie on a certain level.

I don't wanna say it would not have been different if there were no women because it did make a difference. Just to see it. I think modeling, being able to see someone who, for the most part, was—we shared the same gender, doing something that I am trying to do. It's helpful, but I felt like I got no extra support from that particular person. Absolutely not.

You know, I have been on sessions where I assisted, and the clients would come in and greet everybody except me because I was the only woman, thinking that maybe, I guess, that I am whoever, and then when I went to the patch bay to plug stuff and they were like, "*Oh, wow!* She's assistant engineer?" I'm like, "Wow," you know? But once again, you can't react to that. You have to remain professional. So they just thought I was somebody hanging out.

Hillary Johnson: Sure, yeah. Definitely. The place where I worked in the '90s where I was the manager, two out of three assistants were women because I hired them. [Laughs] Almost all the records I did in the '90s were with women assistants. Then beyond that, I worked with women techs in my jobs, where I am a tech. I've worked with other females, like live sound engineers. When I am doing live sound, all—it's pretty much all the time.

The people that have said anything have been like, "This is actually pretty cool, having women around." I've been told that it's really great and refreshing to have women in the studio. So most men that I encounter, even if they are, like, the really burly kind, I think that they like the idea that there's a different chemistry, especially if they are singing about love and they are singing to a dude? Like, they don't want to do that. It helps them with the performance! So the only commentary I've gotten about that is positive.

Sylvia Massy: Well, I think that sometimes musicians, definitely the harder, crusty, rock guys, kinda tiptoe around me. They maybe feel a little conscious cursing or just being themselves around me because I'm a girl. But I try to get rid of that right away just by yelling at them.

So, the other thing that I found was, when I work with women musicians, that we have a tremendous bond just for the fact that we're kinda rarities in the studio anyway. So for instance, I worked with a band called Thunderpussy recently, and they're kind of a noise-rock band from Seattle, and it's an all-girl band, and they play the hell out of their instruments, and the singer is great, and we just had more fun than anyone in the studio, especially just because we were a bunch of girls goofing off, making a bunch of noise. And maybe there was something especially fun about that just because they were so much like me; they're, like, dedicated to making noise and living that lifestyle. That was especially fun working with those girls. I do enjoy working on women's music. I hate to say that phrase, though [in air quotes] "women's music." Lame.

> **Kallie Marie:** Do you have any experiences of working with a female engineer or having other women on the production side with you?

Sylvia Massy: That's a good question. You know, actually, I have only worked with a few women engineers, and one of them that I really liked was Lori Castro, and we did records together up here in California. But now she works in LA; she's doing really well in Los Angeles, working on films. But, yeah, it's so unusual for a woman to be working in a studio that I rarely see them! So it's kinda weird like that. It's actually much worse than it was in the '70s and '80s. There were more women working in the studios in the '70s and '80s, but now I think that there's just other opportunities that women are more interested in, and it's kind of sad. Yeah, that's what it is.

> **Kallie Marie:** How do you think that's impacted you, then, not having other women on the technical side with you? Do you feel that that's impacted you at all, either professionally or personally, in your day-to-day work?

Sylvia Massy: No. I mean, I kind of have always worked with guys, so it doesn't really even come to my mind. Yeah, it's not really an issue. However, it would be nice for more women to be involved, but this has not really been an issue. I just don't see that many. It's weird. What I have noticed is in the schools that there are a lot of women interested in the field of engineering or production, and I meet a lot of them when

I do lectures at universities. I meet a lot of women, and they are really gung-ho, but I don't know if they are making it out in the world. I keep track of some of them, but yeah, it's something that—it's a career that you spend a lot of time getting your feet under you, and maybe in ten years before you start making money. How many people can even wait that long? I think that women get discouraged, as well as men. Everybody['s] discouraged, and so, like, if there's a hundred people who graduate a program for recording and production, you know, maybe twenty of them will have solid jobs, and if the percentage of one hundred people of women is just 10 percent, then we are looking at two people, two women. So, you know, you're just gonna just gradually see less because it's just a very hard job to break into, and it takes a long time to make money, and you just gotta love it. That's the only thing: You can't get into it for fame or for money. You have to get into it because you love music. That should be number one.

Johnette Napolitano: If I had to have that many people around me ever again to make a record, I wouldn't do it. Whoever still has the money to work this way must be worth it, in which case they hire their own team anyway. That's up to the artist, then.

Let me tell you, when I booked the sessions as studio manager at Gold Star Studios, I learned something very important: The only name on that purchase order that mattered was the artist. It's not the producer's name up on that marquee sweating about ticket sales; it's the artist. The producer doesn't get the bad reviews, even though the production might: a matter of fan taste, like Willie Nelson making a reggae record.

Kerry Pompeo: I haven't! That would be pretty cool. You know, I've kind of tossed around the idea of having an all-girl studio, but again, that would just, kind of—it's, again, being too all-chick, you know? It's not reality, and it's not a good mix for art? You need all those diverse-nesses there. I think it's about diversity. Diversity brings the best out of anything. I mean look at these Fortune 500 companies that want to be all one-pane, one- dimension when there's many dimensions and many facets; that's when it's taking the best of what everybody does and elevating it as a whole.

> **Kallie Marie:** It's kind of fascinating, though, because you and I can sit here and say that we don't want anything to be all of one thing, and yet we've never experienced what is the norm for so many men, which is that it's very often all of them.

Kerry Pompeo: I never even thought about that. Like, that's just the normal.

> **Kallie Marie:** Have you had any experiences at all where there was more than one woman that you got to work with, specifically in the studio? Where you had an intern that was another woman? Or a woman above you?

Kerry Pompeo: Well, I've hired women interns, so working with them has always been great. I enjoy, like, giving them the opportunity, but I don't see them as being any[thing], off the bat. When someone is an intern, it's a very level playing field, men and women. Maybe I've just been using my discretion as to who I hire, too. But I've always inter-viewed equally—and maybe not even equally. Maybe if I saw a girl's résumé come through, I just would want to meet them anyway, just to give them a shot.

Ebonie Smith: I think what I have noticed over my career is role designating and role management. When you are working on a pretty robust project, I think the key is just making sure that the people you're working with are professional. When people are professional, they know how to play the role that's been assigned to them. I don't know that it's necessarily a thing of, that says, "More women on the team means that there's more respect. [Laughs] More guys on the team means that there's less respect of boundaries." Obviously, that can happen with people that are just unprofessional, and I've always worked with really professional people, and I've always, at the top levels . . . I've seen just how well a project can run when everybody is professional and understands their role and sticks to that role.

The best example I can give is working on *Hamilton*, just seeing how well-oiled their machine was: Engineers came in every day, the composer—I was assistant engineer, a mixing engineer, and a tracking/comping engineer, and they just worked so seamlessly because everybody was professional. I was the only woman on the team, but you didn't see the guys stepping all on me, and I wasn't stepping all on them; they weren't stepping on each other. And that's, without question, the most successful project that I have ever worked on. So I think it's really more of a thing of professionalism versus whether or not they are guys or girls. I noticed a lot of stepping on toes when they are young guys and young girls who haven't really worked on enough and haven't really . . . come up in the proper studio training systems; they don't really know how to be on a team. So I've noticed with the younger up-and-coming, even with some of my interns, and it's my job to teach them how to be a producer if you've been hired to be a producer, an engineer if you've been hired to be an engineer, and there are professional ways to move up and to bounce from role to role. But you have to, in a professional way, do the job that you've been hired to do. So, yeah.

Kallie Marie: Have you had the experience of having more than one woman on your team besides yourself?

Ebonie Smith: Yeah, that's something I always enjoy—working with other women. There's a different energy; there's more camaraderie. For whatever reason, the conversations in the studio are a lot more interesting and a lot more relatable. Over time, it's just been a wonder-ful experience of having more than one woman on my team. I guess the thing that's interesting to me is how easily women kind of bind together to create what we don't have and to be a support system for each other. It's almost instant, for whatever reason; it's an instant con-nection, from what I have noticed, when it comes to team building. So, and I don't know, maybe that has to do with the dynamics of the women I work with, but I've never really had any issues, and truth-fully, I haven't worked with as many women as men, but the women I've worked with, it's always nice, and I always have such a good time working [with women].

Kallie Marie: When you've had a team that's made up of more than one woman, how was this received by clients?

Ebonie Smith: It's been received the same. You know, I haven't seen any weirdness ever, and I probably, over my career, have done five hundred or so sessions at the major-label level. So I've had male interns, female interns—I've never seen anything where an all-female team was met with any. . . fear, I guess you can say. Then again, I can only perceive so much. I never had anybody outwardly tell me that or outwardly express that, so who knows what's lurking behind the surface? But it's never come up to me personally—like, "Oh, I am concerned that these women can't do it," or "I am concerned that, you know." I've never been approached like that. I don't have any specific incidences.

I think my situation is very unique, too, because I work in-house at one of the biggest labels in the world, so when people come into the studio where I am, I am introduced as the person who runs the space. So—and our studio is in the office—people are typically on their best behavior when they come to the studio at [label name omitted]. So I don't really know what women are experiencing if they're working at different studios that are their own entity, but my studio is literally around the corner from the CEO of our label. So people feel like they have to be respectful. And it hasn't always—when I wasn't working at a studio like that, people weren't always so respectful. So I think it also depends on the space and the environment you are in, what type of clients come to that studio, as well. There are a lot of factors that could determine how women are actually treated at their place of business . . . I'm just making an observation that may influence why I've never had certain issues at the office.

> **Kallie Marie:** If you've had other issues before, then that's interesting, too, because that does shed light on your hypothesis. Because if your experience has changed as your career has developed, then you know that definitely says something about that: as you progressed, your experiences have gotten better, perhaps for a variety of reasons.

Ebonie Smith: I still have, outside of the label system, people who don't believe that I'm the person I say I am. I went to a holiday party last year down at a pretty big studio [in] downtown Manhattan, and I was put on the list by an engineer friend of mine who works down there. And I get down there, and I am not on the list. So I'm like, "Dude, you know I told you I was coming down. What's going on?" So I try texting him, but because he's running around, like, he can't text me back, and so the guy at the front desk is like, "You're not on the list." And I am like, "Well, can you call this guy?" And he's like, "You gotta text him or something so he can come down and let you up." I was like, "Well, um, okay . . ." So I wait for a while, and then somebody comes down, and maybe I misheard it, but I don't think so. I heard someone go, "[Label omitted] engineer is here. [Label omitted] engineer," and not, you know, "Who else could that be?" So I go up to try to get in, and I'm like, "I heard somebody say, '[Label omitted] engineer'; that's me." And he goes, "Really? You are?" So, it's like, "Okay . . ." You know, at that point, I just left.

So I still have these experiences. Part of it is that this city is full of people that are full of shit; part of it for me just comes from that. The other part I think does have to do with my gender, and it may have to do with my race, as well. It may have to do with the fact that I look younger than I am. There are lots of reasons why people discriminate against you: They don't think you fit the look of what they [are] expecting, and maybe he would have done that to anybody and would have done it to any guy that was down there. Like, I am an [label omitted] engineer! Who knows! I don't know.

But that has happened to me, and before I was even working there, at [label omitted], you know, you have the burden of proof, and I've always taken it as, it's hard for everybody, so I'm not going to take it personally. Like, this industry is hard for everybody, male or female. Like, if you want to be a top producer or a top engineer, you've got to prove it to people, and that's on you. That's nobody's job to prove that you're great; it's you. So I haven't harped on it too deeply, though—like, "I'm not getting opportunities because I am a woman or because I am Black." It's like, "Whatever, I don't care," like, "Let me get going with what I need to do so that I am getting the work and I'm getting the opportunities." And, like I said before, in the previous question, like, it's about what I am doing, about "I am getting paid," making sure I get to be working on the records I deserve to be working on and want to be working on. You can keep your stereotypes, and you can call me what you want—I really don't care, like, as long as I am getting where I need to go professionally and the people that know that I am Ebonie Smith from [label omitted] know that. You know, and that's kind of how I approach it.

Andrea Yankovsky: Occasionally, occasionally. Rare. Like, when I was on staff at a studio, it was very rare to have outside team members come in, such as producer, engineer, to have more than one woman aside from myself. I was really lucky in that I was working at Power Station/Avatar. Zoe [Thrall] was managing, and she—one of her strengths was that she just made gender a nonissue for running the business, and so there were female assistants and female PAs, and she was just like, "I don't care what gender you are. Period. End of story. End of conversation." Which is fantastic. So when projects would be staffed with multiple assistants, there were women. But in terms of an outside independent coming in, I can count on one hand the number of female engineers and producers. Yeah, now that I think about it. But actually, no, it also depended on genre, too. There were more women in, like, classical and jazz, but that may also have been the nature of the studios at the time. I can't say that it was a totally representative sample. You know what I mean? There were some producers, usually not engineers. In terms of engineers, I can think of basically two or three female engineers.

Kallie Marie: How was this, in your experience, received by clients?

Andrea Yankovsky: I think, for the most part, it depended on what the woman's role was. So when a woman was coming in as an engineer, she was usually hired by the client. So again, there was the sort of transition. I came in when there was a transition, where the staff engineers were starting to become a totally lost breed. So people were going independent, and so everybody was having to hire their own engineers and producers or working with the label. So that was a choice, you know—would there be assistants? Or the PAs were women, and sometimes you would get comments or whatever. But for the most part, your job as an assistant is to disappear. So if you are doing your job well, they shouldn't be noticing you.

Anonymous: I think when you are the only woman on the team, sometimes you get treated or feel like the token or the unicorn with special powers and there's a bit more pressure because you feel you are representing all women in that space. So whether you make a mistake or do something great, it can feel like it will be interpreted as a reflection of the competency of all women in that role. When there is a whole team of women, your gender is not as noticed, and there is not as much pressure to uphold or shatter a stereotype.

In my experience, clients receive this better because they have no other choice. When there are other men around and you're the only woman, the client often assumes you are not in the technical role and will automatically approach or defer to the male coworker. When there is a team of women or several women, they have no choice but to talk to a woman, and there is less resistance.

2

WOMEN AS PRODUCERS AND ENGINEERS

Taking into consideration the daily professional lives of these engineers, I wanted to look at circumstances underpinning their work experiences in the recording studio that had been in many cases categorically societally influenced. (This is not to say that any of the issues discussed in the preceding chapter or the rest of this book is not in some way or other a societal construct.) In this chapter I have termed the *politeness perception* to describe the expectation that in certain instances women are to always be pleasant, polite, kind, nurturing, and so on. As Rebecca Solnit explains, "Women get to keep a wider range of emotional possibility [than men], though they are stigmatized for expressing some of the fiercer ones, the feelings that aren't ladylike and deferential, and so much else: ambition, critical intelligence, independent analysis, dissent, anger" (Solnit 2017, 29). This stereotype works for and against women depending on the scenario, and here I wanted to delve into and explore it as it may be experienced by these women in the recording studio and industry.

The role of a producer can be one of nurture and can also be one of hard-core business negotiation. Depending on which side of this stereotype a person may find themself falling on that day, this politeness perception can be a hindrance or a help. This ties into a later exploration about some attitudes that are held about what women's "natural" aptitudes are seen to be—otherwise known as *biological predeterminism*, these presumptions can both be helpful and hurtful, depending on the scenario. Furthermore, women's own self-awareness of some of these stereotypes may affect them in different ways, and I was curious as to how they saw these dynamics between themselves and their clients.

As with some stereotypes, occasionally there are positive associations with the politeness perception, but the negatives generally outweigh them, because it puts people in a box. Commonly held descriptive biases can hold women back during the hiring process. For example, journalist Eric Jaffe writes,

> [Descriptive stereotype] ascribes certain characteristics to women. They are caring, warm, deferential, emotional, sensitive, and so on— traits consistently used to describe women for decades. Left alone those traits aren't bad, of course, but when a woman performs a job traditionally held by men they can become incredibly harmful.
>
> The result is what psychologist Madeleine E. Heilman of New York University calls a "lack of fit" between the personality a woman is supposed to possess and the attributes considered necessary for the job. (Jaffe 2014)

Furthermore, substantial research finds that there is no innate gender-predicated proclivity for behaviors like kindness, organization, or being technical. Rather, such traits are adaptive and are shaped by early childhood development, education, and cultural environments as well as social norms. Even still, should a woman be at the helm as either engineer or producer, her contributions may be viewed as less significant. To this point, Björk has said that, even as an artist who contributes to the production process and technical aspects of her music, her contributions are viewed as less. In an interview with Jessica Hopper, writing for *Pitchfork* in 2015, Björk commented,

> I didn't want to talk about that kind of thing for 10 years, but then I thought, "You're a coward if you don't stand up. Not for you, but

for women. Say something." So around 2006 I put something on my website where I cleared something up, because it'd been online so many times that it was becoming a fact. It wasn't just one journalist getting it wrong, *everybody* was getting it wrong. I've done music for, what, *30 years*? I've been in the studio since I was eleven; Alejandro [Ghersi] had never done an album when I worked with him. He wanted to put something on his own Twitter, just to say it's coproduced. I said, "No, we're never going to win this battle. Let's just leave it." But he insisted. [Ghersi came out as nonbinary in 2018 and began using she/her pronouns.] I've sometimes thought about releasing a map of all my albums and just making it clear who did what. But it always comes across as so defensive that, like, it's pathetic. I could obviously talk about this for a long time. . . .

I have nothing against Kanye West. Help me with this—I'm not dissing him—this is about how people talk about him. With the last album he did, he got all the best beatmakers on the planet at the time to make beats for him. A lot of the time, he wasn't even there. Yet no one would question his authorship *for a second*. If whatever I'm saying to you now helps women, I'm up for saying it. For example, I did 80 percent of the beats on *Vespertine*, and it took me *three years* to work on that album, because it was all microbeats—it was like doing a huge embroidery piece. Matmos came in the last two weeks and added percussion on top of the songs, but they didn't do any of the main parts, and they are credited *everywhere* as having done the whole album. [Matmos'] Drew [Daniel] is a close friend of mine, and in every single interview he did, he corrected it. And they don't even listen to him. It really is strange. . . .

I have to say—I got a feeling I am going to win in the long run, but I want to be part of the zeitgeist, too. I want to support young girls who are in their twenties now and tell them: *You're not just imagining things*. It's tough. Everything that a guy says once, you have to say five times. Girls now are also faced with different problems. I've been guilty of one thing: After being the only girl in bands for ten years, I learned—the hard way—that if I was going to get my ideas through, I was going to have to pretend that they—men—had the ideas. I became really good at this and I don't even notice it myself. I don't really have an ego. I'm not that bothered. I just want the whole thing to be good. And I'm not saying one bad thing about the guys who were with me in the bands, because they're all amazing and creative, and they're doing incredible things now. But I come from a generation where *that* was the only way to get things done. So I have to play stupid and just do everything with five times the amount of energy, and then it will come through.

When people don't credit me for the stuff I've done, it's for several reasons. I'm going to get very methodical now! [Laughs] One! I learned what a lot of women have to do is make the guys in the room think it was *their* idea, and then you back them up. Two! I spend 80 percent of the writing process of my albums on my own. I write the melodies. I'm by the computer. I edit a lot. That for me is very solitary. I don't want to be photographed when I'm doing that. I don't invite people around. The 20 percent of the album process when I bring in the string orchestras, the extras, that's documented more. That's the side people see. When I met M.I.A., she was moaning about this, and I told her, "Just photograph yourself in front of the mixing desk in the studio, and people will go, 'Oh, okay! A woman with a tool, like a man with a guitar.'" Not that I've done that much myself, but sometimes you're better at giving people advice than doing it yourself. I remember seeing a photo of Missy Elliott at the mixing desk in the studio and being like, *a-ha!*

It's a lot of what people *see*. During a show, because there are people onstage doing the other bits, I'm *just a singer*. For example, I asked Matmos to play all the beats for the *Vespertine* tour, so maybe that's kind of understandable that people think they made them. So maybe it's not *all* sexist evil. [Laughs] But it's an ongoing battle. I hope it doesn't come across as too defensive, but it is the truth. I definitely can feel the third or fourth feminist wave in the air, so maybe this is a good time to open that Pandora's box a little bit and air it out. (Hopper 2015, emphases original)

Björk's experiences and comments on this phenomenon inter-weave both descriptive bias and prescriptive biases as well as her in-credibly astute self-awareness around the importance of visibility. (I had hoped to speak to both Björk and Imogen Heap during my early stages of research, as both are self-producing artists with substantial music-production backgrounds.)

Here I have asked these women to reflect on how they dealt with wielding power in the studio, the times when they used the politeness perception to their benefit or times they specifically didn't, and, in gen-eral, whether they had reflected on these experiences in this way before now. (One difficulty in conducting these interviews is that, while these women are engineers, not all of them are academics, and so sometimes they weren't familiar with a specific term or concept that I threw at them. Thus these interviews were in some instances their first exposure to some concepts and their first opportunity to reflect on them, which is okay. They've been busy being engineers and producers, not academics in fields outside their own.)

"When it comes to family and working life, the biological rule seems to be that there were never any rules. While the realities of child-birth and lactation are fixed, culture and environment can dictate how women live just as much as their bodies do," writes Angla Saini in her book *Inferior: How Science Got Women Wrong—and the New Research That's Rewriting the Story* (2017, 119). Since biology seems to be a men-tal roadblock for some people, this study wouldn't be complete without a discussion of a woman's choice to have children or not. There are, of course, a variety of personal, economic, societal, and cultural fac-tors that go into these decisions. In the United States, unlike in other wealthy nations, there is not a lot of support for maternity leave, or paternity leave for that matter, especially for those in creative fields or for those self-employed. (Despite my best efforts, I was unable to get in-terviewees from other countries in time!) This lack of parental support is even more pervasive for recording engineers and record producers, as

in the United States, we do not often have the health care and benefits provided by some music industry jobs. (Freelance or self-employed
persons, to clarify for readers outside the United States, usually do not
have health care. However, a person might have health care if they work
for a record label, but as discussed earlier, this is not likely the case for
recording engineers and producers.)

For many in the music industry, whether or not to have children
can be a difficult choice because of the long hours and the very strange
schedules. That said, people at NASA or those who work in medicine
have variable hours too, and they somehow manage. They are perhaps
greater supported by structured worker benefits. Chiefly, I wanted to
ask these women about their choices, because there are plenty of men
in the recording industry who have children, so it's clearly not impossible to be a parent and work in this field. What does this look like for
women in the recording industry? How were their careers impacted
by their choices? Did people assume, as is sometimes the case in other
sectors, that promoting them wasn't worthwhile because they would
just drop out to eventually have kids? I wanted to find out which of the
women I spoke with did have kids, and how it worked for them, and
which didn't, and if that had been a conscious decision.

What was also interesting, and I didn't anticipate this—was their
shared sense of "otherness." Many mentioned throughout the course
of the interviews that there was no one else like them, and yet here are
eight of them, all quite similar, and there are plenty more out there, myself included. While this is a small sampling of stories, there are many
common threads. In some instances, it is interesting to note that this
sense of otherness, may be a coping mechanism, or in some cases a point
of pride. In other cases it is shunned, where the people interviewed just
wanted to be part of the "boys' club" or hoped that no one would notice
that they were women. This is a theme that will be discussed later but
came up as soon as we began talking about child-rearing.

Many of the women spoke on being "not like other women" because of their lack of desire for children, and although some of the women interviewed here are indeed parents, many more of them are not and do not want to be. So it would seem that, at least among this small sample, it's not actually that unique to be a woman in this field and not want children. Rather, women wanting or having children already, were a minority in this field. Perhaps now rather than "other," the narrative can be "just like us or me." It is hoped that this will be helpful in unifying and normalizing these choices for people working in this field.

At the start we touch on things that are underpinning (and are discussed in greater detail later) why women are burning out in this field or are not sticking around for the full potential duration of their careers. This is not to say that all women do not stay or make it, because clearly these women did, do, or have to varying degrees. (Andrea Yankovsky is now a mother of two and has changed her career to be an intellectual-property attorney, while Abhita Austin has diversified and is also working as a camerawoman.) There are a lot of personal choices to be made, and that is not solely a reflection of sexism or the recording industry. However, it is worth examining some of their daily experiences and reflections with another layer of awareness.

There is a certain level of fatigue that people experience as the result of processing frequent cognitive dissonance as part of their daily lives. I found myself wondering what the cumulative effects would be over time, as people processing cognitive dissonance on multiple levels have their full cognitive abilities taxed to some degree. Cognitive dissonance can be experienced in a variety of ways and is most exemplified when there's a mismatch in attitudes and behaviors, sometimes even expressed in nonverbal cues, experiences, and information. (Think about the person who smokes but knows it causes cancer; every time they smoke, they experience a twinge of cognitive dissonance.) In the

Harvard Business Review Elisabeth Kelan writes, "I identified four ways in which people made sense of this mismatch between their support for gender equality and the denial that it exists in their immediate work environment. The first rationalization," she writes,

> is that gender inequality exists elsewhere, perhaps at another organization such as a competitor or in a different country. The second is based on a historical perspective: gender inequality existed in the past, say twenty years ago, but not today. The third is the claim that gender inequality can't exist anymore because women are now given advantages in organizations. All of the efforts to fix unequal opportunities, the logic goes, have made it far easier for women to succeed. The final way that people reconciled these contradictory beliefs was to strategically ignore gender inequality. When presented with incidents of discrimination they would say that it had nothing to do with gender. (Kelan 2020)

In this essay, Kelan writes of *gender fatigue*, a concept akin to what I have termed *career fatigue*. "Gender inequality," she writes, "is the result of a multitude of small-scale incidents like these that add up over time. Seemingly unimportant events are regularly regarded as small annoyances that don't matter in the bigger picture. And gender fatigue makes these daily incidents essentially invisible" (Kelan 2020).

So in this portion of the interviews, we explore these women's thoughts on microaggressions they may have experienced and the resulting weight of their cumulative fatigue and how it impacts many work and educational situations. It is interesting to note, that during interviews, many of these women had developed their own coping mechanisms, whether consciously or subconsciously, to blot out the repeated minutiae of day-to-day occurrences. (This is much to the point of Kelan's earlier comments, and you can see the range of coping mechanisms displayed as we move through the interviews.)

Apart from trying to ignore some of these microaggressions, some of the people here have also internalized it to a point that they may be convincing themselves they're not experiencing it all (almost self-gaslighting)—when they do experience it, because it's the only way to handle the cognitive dissonance and move past it. Obviously, this takes a lot of strength and determination, but it becomes an extra cognitive load to carry and an extra barrier that can hinder one's fullest potential cognitive function. I found myself wondering if consistent and long-term experiences of microaggression were contributing factors to burn-out or career fatigue and could be indirectly contributing to the low numbers of women in audio and music production. Are they burning out due to isolation and microaggressions? Are they simply getting out, like anyone in any field, after giving it a serious go for ten to fifteen years (as Sylvia Massy stated, it takes about ten years to start making money in this career) of not getting very far? Are there fewer women because there is a level of fatigue from constantly fighting their way in? (This is not to say it's an easy industry for anyone, so this is an added layer to mentally process, withstand, and find ways to overcome.)

How big of a factor this extra cognitive load is remains to be seen. Can we learn from this discussion, and will we see more women not only stay in the industry longer but also flourish if some of these microaggressions drop away? If we know more about what some of these microaggressions look like, hopefully we can develop the language to discuss them and eventually dismantle them.

Finally, as we as a society and industry clear these roadblocks, what tactics and tools are available to people in these situations? How can we support and build pathways around these microaggressions and take steps to consciously overcome and correct them? It is hoped that by highlighting the microaggressions, potentially one of the last major professional hurdles these women face, allies can be more aware of things that are unrecognized, even if well intentioned. The cumulative load of these small indignities may or may not be on purpose but do have a lasting impact on the people experiencing them.

"NICE GIRLS" AND THE POLITENESS PERCEPTION

Because women are often perceived, or expected to be "nicer," more polite, better communicators, helpful, sensitive, and nurturing. How does this impact women's work as producers and engineers? Are female engineers more common than female producers, and is this an extension of the politeness perception, where women are often seen to be "suited" for helpful, supportive roles? What are your experiences and observations with this?

Abhita Austin: I feel like it's been beneficial, because artists, I have noticed, men and women, open up more to you. You know what I mean? You're trying to figure out what the artist is about and just connect with the artist as the producer or as the engineer. They feel more comfortable, and I have had male producers tell me that, "Oh, they like to put women engineers or women producers with certain artists. You know that they will open up to them." So that's been a benefit, and I feel that I have learned a lot about men in particular; I know about women, but I have learned a lot about men. I have learned that when the smoke clears men are either definitely just as emotional as women, hands down, or even more. They present it like it's—to me, they present themselves as more emotional than women because, in my experience, they haven't been nurtured to handle their emotions properly. So when the emotions do come forth, it's crazy depending on if, like, they're scared, it will come out very strange. They won't say it, but it will come out as being aloof or passive aggressive, something weird. Or if it comes down to something where they don't have the money financially, it will come back down to the performance of something else. Like, "Oh, you know I'm not, like, whatever, happy with this," but when the smoke clears, it's, "I don't have the money." So, I have noticed that men are concerned with the same things as women, because for whatever reason they open up, and I think that might be because I am a woman producer. They open up in the studio, and they are concerned with exactly the same things. They might be even interested in family, children, all that stuff, and they might be even more emotional. In some cases men are very emotional, and I don't know if it's just artistic men, because we are dealing with artists in the studio, but that's what I have found.

I guess outside of the studio, I see more women producers than engineers, hands down. In the studio system, I don't know if I wanna say "more professional," but I guess more of the industry standard, I see more women engineers. Is it because of that whole "nurturing" role? It could be? I really don't know, because I am thinking about the paths that might lead somebody to become an engineer and then a producer. A lot of times a producer that is coming up in the studio system, you are an engineer, and then you cross over into becoming a producer. I have seen that a lot. Because you can be interning with the angle to produce artists and then start producing. So, I don't know. I don't want to just make up theories.

Hillary Johnson: Well, I think that we probably have a better capability, or a higher capability, of multitasking. I don't know if that translates to the studio necessarily, but I think that if you are the kind of person, regardless of your gender, who has the ability to just step back and just analyze everything that you are going to be able to multitask better. So, if you have a higher capacity to multitasking and you have that ability to use it . . . and I think women may be able to multitask better. I've thought about this, and I've thought about whether or not that may translate to actually hearing differently in terms of, you know, people have the ability to isolate a certain drum or a keyboard or whatever. But maybe there's all the talk about having the ability to hear higher frequencies. There could be something else with the multitasking . . . I don't know . . . I don't know . . . it's just a theory, just a theory.

As far as the nurturing and that sort of aspect, I think that I personally do. It's not that I mother people, but I do give them encouragement, and I tell them when they are doing a good job. I don't know, give a crap when they are singing out of key or the drummer is out of time or something like that. But I think most good professional engineers, male or female, do that anyway. So I don't know if being a woman really or being a man really matters that way.

You know, it's funny, none of the women I have watched work are timid. So, I think it's just one of the personality traits that you have to have to work in this kind of an industry, where you are critiquing someone's art constantly. I mean, for me, I've never—I am a straight shooter. I am just going to tell you the facts. I am not going to sugar coat it, not going to be wishy-washy about it. If I don't know, I am going to tell you I don't know. If I have an opinion about it, that's sort of the way that I've seen other women work, but I've also never really been in a room when another woman is working, doing what I do, and not being the one doing it. So I've only, like—I'm speaking of assistants or live sounds guys being girls, you know . . . Or . . . techs even. I mean, I guess, you know there's definitely times when there's even a woman who's more gruff than me. Then someone calls them a bitch under their breath or whatever, just the way they would call a guy like that an asshole.

Johnette Napolitano: Not really answerable. Those very skills—and they are skills—may get you the job with one artist and not with another.

Kerry Pompeo: Well, I think, as an engineer, as females in this role, we've all encountered, when the band walks into the room and they think that you're another vocalist or you're an artist or you're not somebody that's going to be in that seat. But a lot of people have perceived me as the studio mom. I've never—the overly nice is not something people would ever say, categorize me as, but definitely, like, "studio mom," because I would yell at people if they had to be yelled at, things like that. I always—if they have a stereotype about what I was going to be, I wasn't going to let it be a detrimental one.

I use it to my advantage, because a lot of what I do is [as a] tracking engineer; I need people to be in a very vulnerable state. So, I definitely wanted them to feel comfortable around me, but also that's good customer service. If I knew that the artist likes root beer, the whole refrigerator would be stocked with it. And that's just being able to break down the wall, where you gain their trust and then you can break them and mold them to whatever you need to do. So that when I did need to yell at them they knew that it was coming from a place that was of love and what was for the best of the song rather than being a "bitchy woman." Where if maybe if they didn't see that caring side of me, I wouldn't have been able to do it, because then I would have just been a "bitch." I get bitchy. I do, I do, especially if, like, a musician is being lazy or wanting to take a shortcut or something. I have no qualms with telling you, "You suck," like, "Go home for the night, and let's go back and do it again, because you're not doing it today." I think that's important. It's very important that women don't get looked at as being bitchy if they have to say that, because if somebody of a different gender was in this seat and said that, would you have the same reaction? I think that is, like, a wall that needs to be broken down. I think that is—it just has to do with understanding that we are working with people in their most sensitive moments. I think because women maybe have had the defense up all the time that they feel that they have to be like that. But it's okay to be nurturing; you have to put people in their comfort zone in this seat, when you're in this seat.

I have techniques to let people know that when I'm here this is my domain. The minute they walk in the door, I mean, I've done sessions with hip-hop artists that have guns in their pockets, but they knew they better put a cap on their Hennessy bottle and it better be far away from my gear, and I didn't have to say anything. They just knew that this was a commanding space for me and that they better not F— with me because their project is in my hands. You know, like . . . maybe it's because I am from Queens? You know, but people just kind of knew that walking through that door, who is in control. I think that's a confidence thing, and that's a big thing that women need to work on, is not caring who is walking through that door and being able to rock it with a blindfold on. A lot of that comes from working your ass off, and that knows no gender. That's—I think that's like we were talking before: Don't be afraid to ask questions, because you are going to be in a situation where a client's going to ask you a question and you're not going to know the answer to it, and that gives them a leg up, and that's where it opens the doors for them to think you're a woman and you're inferior, you know, because you don't have the answers. Well, anybody who doesn't have the answers is inferior.

> **Kallie Marie:** I also think that goes back to something that, sadly, [runs] throughout lots of areas, not just music, and it goes through all of history too. There's been a credibility issue with women, to the fact that to this day in some countries women are not considered credible enough to testify in court on their own behalf. So, as long as we are dealing with a somewhat insidious culture of lack of credibility, I think that the, as you were saying, confidence thing, that's part of where that comes from, is because we are, again, self-aware that we may not be considered credible, especially if we falter, for any reason, or if, heaven forbid, our gear should falter, which could happen to anybody.

Kerry Pompeo: Oh, sure! You have to be able to explain it in an intelligent way or, even better, don't even let people know that your gear is faltering. Which is what I do all the time. Shit fails all the time, you know?

Kallie Marie: Well, that may be something [that we should be teaching] while we are training women specifically in production to help them. Everybody needs that, any man or woman, because the gear is always going to take a shit; it's just what technology does best, is fuck up. Knowing how to manage it and how to calmly troubleshoot, whether you're a man or a woman, in the studio is important. But I think especially that's where our confidence—we get nervous because we are already self-aware of the fact that if anything falters people might go, "Pfffft, it's a chick; she doesn't know."

Kerry Pompeo: Totally. I worked in live sound, and I came up, I was fresh out of school, and I was working with legendary jazz artists. I think they had more of a problem that I was young, but also, like, you know, a girl. That was probably something that they might not have ever seen in their sixty-year career, as a jazz musician. It was experiences like that, that I kind of dove head-in. I used to run in the kitchen, because it was a jazz club that serves supper and everything, and there were many nights where I was running to the kitchen and crying because I was a monitor engineer and these guys wouldn't play if they couldn't hear it right and the show would not go on! So there were times when it was, like, "The clock is ticking, and it's, like, twenty minutes in, and they're not happy with the sounds I am giving them, and, god, what do I do?" You finally figure out a way to make it work, and then you go cry in the back with the cooks, you know, where the musicians can't see you.

It's situations like that, that I think we need to not be scared of and challenge ourselves with. That only made me a better engineer; that only made me know how to give a musician the most awesome headphone mix that they are like, "Wow! I'm gonna fucking, like, this is the . . . I've never heard it like this in my headphones! Now I can give a real performance!" But that was from these old jazz musicians putting their foot down and being like, "No, this is my art, and you're not making it sound right, and I'm not playing until it does," and me having to have that pressure of dealing with that. So, [laughs] definitely made me a very good and very aware engineer for headphones and what the musician needs to hear in order to perform accurately.

You have to prove more—that's a fact! That's one thing that I will not deny is that women have to prove more. I am guilty of it. You know, when I hire or interview, I am guilty of it, and I don't like it, and I'm like, "Damn! I just did something that, like, I would have hated if I was sitting in that seat." But it's such a subconscious thing that's ingrained in us.

Ebonie Smith: Well, I think about this all the time, not just because I am a woman, but also because I am Black, you know, so there's this perception that, is that, Black women are angry and hostile. So I feel myself thinking about that a lot and feeling the need to smile more and feeling the need to make sure that my disposition and my countenance is not threatening [or is not] perceived as threatening. And it is exhausting. You know, it really it is. But I recognize that it's a part of the job, any business; this is a service business. When you are an engineer or producer, your job is to make the client feel comfortable. It's not fair that I feel an added pressure when it comes to that because I'm female or because I am Black, but at the same time, everybody should be doing [it]. So, just because guys don't have the same pressure to do it doesn't mean that they shouldn't do it. So I think everybody should smile, everybody should make the effort to be extra nice, because you want the client to bring their business back. Once again, the stereotypes of, like, whatever, "women should be nicer," I've had people tell me that. You know, one of my first experiences working in the studio was in Cameroon. I cut my teeth making records in Africa, working in studios and going around. So the gender issues are way, way more pervasive, and I had a lot of people say, "Hey, you know, you should be cooking. You should be, like, doing—taking care of your man; you shouldn't be

out at the studio, late at night. You should be home by a certain hour."
But you just, like, for me, my perspective is still, like, "I don't hear you."
I'm out here, and I'm going to do what I've been called to do with my
life, and that is to make records, and nothing is getting in the way of
that. Nobody's preconceived notions of what I am capable of, none of
that! Like, I am going to do what I set out to, so if a person's . . . stereotype [is] that I should be nice . . . the reality is just that I am going to
be me. Do I feel pressure to be nice? Yeah, but I think anybody in our
industry as a service provider, engineers, to producers, managers, record
label executives—we all feel that pressure, one way or another, to come
across as pleasant. I think it doesn't take women more, but I think it's
just kind of the nature of the job.

> **Kallie Marie:** Sure, yeah. Well, I guess my thinking of it was actu-
> ally the flip side of that . . . If it's perceived that we're nice because
> we're, like, more gentle or kind or nurturing, what happens when
> this session calls for us to be a bit of a ball-breaker or to be pushy
> or to be aggressive or to [put] our foot down? How is that received
> differently because it's expected that men are going to be that way,
> and, again, how is that different for us in terms of client relation-
> ship if I have to walk up to his face and say, "Hey, you're not playing
> that right" or "Can you do that again?" or "No, I won't accept that"
> or "This is not okay"? Then people can get a bit, like, "Woah!" You
> know, it depends on the client; it depends on the situation. But I
> was curious of everybody's experiences on both sides of that stereo-
> type, because sometimes it works for you, and sometimes it works
> against you, and, like you've said, there's a whole different aspect for
> you regarding race as well, so I think, you know, that everything ties
> in, and it doesn't live in a bubble?

Ebonie Smith: You know what, though? I am glad that you clarified
that, because there is a side of it that is—I think it's important for
women to be stern. I have interns, and I have worked with artists and

clients where I do have to step in and be stern. I don't have a problem with it. I have more of a problem with, like, the niceness. I don't have a problem with, "That sounds like garbage." That's the least of my problems; that's easy for me to do that. My struggle was softening the blow. Like, what helps me not to be like, "That sucks!" But you do have to be stern at times, and I think [what] helps me do that is being good, cause you have to establish respect. I think once you establish respect because you are good, when you tell somebody, "That's whack," they respect it, and they trust your ability. So, right now I have some interns, got a bunch of guys, you know, there's three of them, and the first day, couple days, they came in and then they saw just how much I know, so now I can't do anything without them asking me, over and over and over, "Is this good? Is this Good? What do you think?" Like they want my perspective because they respect my ability. So I feel like most women, if you come in freaking badass, you don't have to worry about somebody being like, "Please don't say anything to me," or "Who is this woman saying something to me?" They respect your opinion because you are good. Then I think it is just that less complicated when it is time to step up and be like, "This is what it is." It is all about trust. In my philosophy, there are ways to establish trust, but the easiest way to establish trust is just to be hella good, as good as you can be.

Andrea Yankovsky: I think there's two categories, because a producer's role is at the very least a dual role—you have a business role, and you have a creative role. I think that in terms of their gender issues in each role is totally different. When you're trying to get a performance out of somebody, that can often really work for you in terms of [politeness perception], again, if the artist is the one who hired you. That's a really big deal. It also kinda depends on the person that you wanna be and what your kind of beliefs are of how you should be or how you want to be. So, it depends on who hires you, but that in and of itself is the salient point: Who is gonna hire you? What do people in the industry perceive about you? What's your reputation? And, at the end of the day, I think you do what works for you, as a producer, in terms of the artistic side. In terms of the business side, that's an interesting side, because, again, that goes more to perceptions of women in business, of the differences between being assertive versus being aggressive and how you conduct yourself. Again, on the artist side, the numbers are much more equal in terms of who you are dealing with. I am not saying that they are equal, but there are certainly more women artists than there were when I was really active in the industry; there weren't a lot more women artists than there were, say, women producers or women engineers and label execs, and so, in terms of even roles in the labels, I'd be curious to know what percentage of jobs in the labels women were getting—whether they were jobs that were more stereotypically female jobs.

Kallie Marie: That's kind of the second part of this question, in a way. Is that because of this *politeness perception*, as I am calling it? Are women more often seen to be better "suited"—I am saying in air quotes—for helpful or supportive roles? Is it more common to see assistants and assistant engineers than producers that are women because it is a supporting role or studio managers and things like that are more clerical or what I like to call *glorified secretarial*, the sort of admin kind of roles, which are equally important? Is it more common for women to be in that sort of role, like as a journalist or running the studio and taking care of organizing things and communications, as opposed to doing technical and/or artistic things or being the leading producer on projects?

Andrea Yankovsky: It's a chicken-and-an-egg thing too, because it's also jobs. Honestly, I went from an engineering role to a studio-management role, and I did not [do it] because I was better suited toward organization; but one of the things behind the decision was I wanted to learn the business side, but, two, I also didn't want the crazy hours. [Laughs] At that point, I was—I think I was really burnt on just working, working, working all the time, and I wanted something, at least for a little while, that was more structured, a little more steady, a little more . . . nine-to-five. Frankly, I found that personally to be too boring, but you have to try it out to find out. And at that point I didn't have a family, but I could totally see it was definitely factoring into my calculations, where, well, okay, if I did have a family, how do you deal with childcare issues?

Anonymous: I think these stereotypical traits of women for the most part would be more advantageous as a producer than an engineer—particularly, for example, being communicative. I don't know for sure, but I would guess that there are more female engineers than female producers, at least of those I personally know. But I don't think this is part of the politeness perception. I see a producer as more of a nurturing role and engineer [as] more of a technical, button-pushing role, which is definitely considered less feminine. However, being more communicative and nurturing as a woman has, I think, helped me be a better and more popular, successful engineer than stereotypical men who can be a little colder and less approachable.

I think part of the reason there are so few women producers, in addition to [its] being a historically male job, is that the title "producer" is so general, in some ways it's hard to define what a producer does, and people have different definitions of what a producer is. I think, in general, men are more willing to "fake it 'til you make it" and make some beats at home and call themselves producers. Whereas, not always, but mostly I see women being more humble and not able to give themselves a title until they feel they've accomplished something or proven themselves in the industry in some way.

Plus, in general, men get more assumed credit for knowing more, whereas often a woman has to prove she knows what she's talking about. Or, conversely, when a woman is the token engineer, then it is assumed that she is exceptionally special (the unicorn phenomenon), and if she performs average, then it is perceived as disappointing, even if her performance was the same as a man's. This is one example of how I've seen proof that a woman has to work twice as hard for the same recognition.

REFLECTIONS ON THE NOTION OF CHILDBEARING AND -REARING WHILE WORKING IN A STUDIO ENVIRONMENT

A personal question: How has the notion of children affected or not affected your work as a producer? What assumptions have people made with regard to this? How is this different for men do you think? How can this be made to be more balanced—this being a wider social issue that does impact women in all career categories?

Abhita Austin: I don't want to have any kids, so it's not really affected [me].

> **Kallie Marie:** Have people made any assumptions about that in relation to you working in music? Have there been any places in your career where people have made an assumption about that? Something like, "You're probably going to have kids, so you're not going to be able to do this job for very long . . ." that kind of thing?

Abhita Austin: No, I don't think so! Not that I know of. I am sure that something's affected me, but I don't directly know of it. I am not aware of it because I haven't experienced it. But I am also aware, like, a vibration, that, you know, even though we don't hear it, it's affecting us. So, even though I don't see it or experience it, there's that collective consciousness that's affecting me. So I am aware of that.

> **Kallie Marie:** Well, that could be more of a societal thing, and anything that we do is perceived as temporary because it is often assumed that we are eventually going to go be mothers. That's not to say that everybody thinks that; but there is always an element

that it might be thought, "Do this for now . . . but eventually . . ." There's this "eventually," even if you say, "But I am not interested in eventually!" Then there's a whole other conversation that starts . . . "You'll change your mind, you'll change your mind . . ."

Abhita Austin: You've had that happen to you?

Kallie Marie: Oh, constantly. Somebody told me once in the studio that I wouldn't last long, because I was cute and I would definitely end up pregnant. And I was like, "Well I have control of those things." You know?? And they said, "But it will happen; it will just happen." And I was like, "It's not like the divine hand of god [laughs] is just going to [makes noise] Pshhhpoof!"

Abhita Austin: It is bizarre that someone is just going to come at your face, "You are cute, and you are going to end up pregnant." Wow.

Leslie M. G. Bird: Did you see that Sound Girls event in LA, where I was making this argument, that, male or female, the problem isn't the career, the problem is childcare? The argument that I made at the camp, I think, is salient: if you're a doctor or a bricklayer or whatever, an officer, and you have kids, you have to have an understanding with your spouse or significant other or family about childcare arrangements. I think it's interesting that women were sort of hanging onto my every word. I feel like people are frightened, you know, that we are going to ban the studio from 8 p.m. to 2 a.m.! "How can you have this lifestyle?" And I urge the women who think we'll have . . . any lifestyle, that have kids, whatever—you still need somebody to quit, so the question: Is it different for guys in audio? You could say that because there are more men in audio, and even if those men have children, you sort of assumed that the wife is home taking care of the kids. "The kids are with my spouse." Because that's what people with kids do. They have childcare arrangements.

Kallie Marie: What things can we do to support women with children, or what things in your experience do you feel would have helped you?

Leslie M. G. Bird: I don't think it's an industry-specific problem.

Kallie Marie: No, of course not. I just wanted to know about your experience and what you feel would have helped you. Thinking about your own experiences, what would have been useful to you, or what is your opinion?

Leslie M. G. Bird: I have two kids, and my husband works from home, and our kids are enrolled in school, so during the day I can do whatever I need to do, and my kids go to school. So that's my experience. So, I'm good. I don't know about other people's experiences. I am able to do what I do because I make enough money to have them taken care of during the day.

Kallie Marie: Do you think that your husband working from home helps in this situation?

Leslie M. G. Bird: No. I think that the fact that, you know, if I do have an evening gig, or even an appointment, the fact that he's okay taking care of the kids makes it easier for me.

Hillary Johnson: No, because I have never wanted them. The only thing that's been different for me is the relationship thing, because for the first, I dunno, up until the past seven or eight years, I was always very single. Even [if] I was dating someone, I was still very single. So I devoted myself to work, work, work, work, work, which is very male. It's very male to do that. And then only in the past six or so years have I been in a committed relationship, and my boyfriend's very supportive. But I know that he's like, "Why are you always working, working,

working, or traveling, or going to Prague, or going here, or doing this, or whatever?" So the kids thing is a nonissue, but trying to adjust to being a workaholic, in a field that I am passionate about, has been challenging, only more recently, because of the relationship thing.

Do I think it's different [for men]? Yes, I think because just as a society we are used to the men being the ones that are always gone. So I think a family—if a couple wanted to have a family, then the expectation is that the woman is going to stay at home and raise them. But, you know, there are a lot of stay-at-home dads now. There are a lot of nannies. So I do think it's different for men, but I think that it's not as different as, or would be as obvious, or would be something that we would assume.

I think a woman who wants to have kids is a whole different kind of woman than me. So—and I don't even have any kind of anything; it is just a totally different thing. I can't imagine that a woman who would want to have a kid would want to have a career as passionately as I do. I am probably wrong; there's probably women out there who want both, and if they do want both, they are probably the kind of woman who knows how to juggle them both. I couldn't imagine, you know, I am juggling the relationship and the career and it's challenging, so I can't imagine trying to juggle something else too. Foowf!

Sylvia Massy: Oh, now, this is a big one, because this type of job, in this job, I was kind of given a choice at one point when I was just getting some success. I had just worked with Rick Rubin, and I had just recorded the *System of a Down* record, and I had a lot of jobs ahead of me, and I also had a studio at Sound City, in Los Angeles. I had the B room; I had all the equipment. And all the sudden I was thirty-seven years old, and I had to make a choice: Am I going to continue with my career, or am I going to go have babies? And pretty much the two things couldn't happen at the same time, not with this type of job. So

I had to make a decision. And I decided to go have babies, and I quit Los Angeles, and moved to a little town called Weed, where I had a relationship with a fellow, got married, and we decided to have babies. But, unfortunately, I had waited too long. So no babies when you are thirty-eight to thirty-nine years old. I had already reached the point of no return with the children, and the idea of adoption was a difficult one for my husband; he wasn't going to go for that. So I started doing recording up in the little town of Weed. I built a studio, and one room turned to two, and two rooms turned to five, and I had a big production studio up there. Because I had made the decision, "I'm not having babies— I can't have babies," I just went full bore into my career.

So, here's a big issue, and that's my personal story, but this is a big issue with anyone, in these types of entertainment jobs that require you to dedicate your life to your career: . . . at one point you're going to have to make a decision on whether you're going to go continue with your career or stop and go have a family and maybe pick it up later. I do know a couple women who have left the industry. Trina Shoemaker is one. She left the industry for a short time so that she could have children, and now she's back, and she's really a go-getter, one of the people that I admire the most because she's made it work. But, yeah, it's a painful story for a lot of women who have to make the choice, and that's part of the reason that I believe there's not that many women in these types of jobs, because you need to have social interaction, you need to have the idea of having a family and be moving in that direction. It's a basic human urge for all of us, but this type of work will restrict your being able to have a family, for sure. There was one other thing: you know, ultimately, it seems like a sad story, but for me, I am very happy with how my life has turned out. I have no regrets about not having had children, and I live an amazing life where I get to do what I want, and actually, considering how many bands I have worked with, I have hundreds of children. Hundreds of children. And I continue to be in contact with them, you know, every day. So, I have lost nothing for not having a family. And if there's any message to give to any young people, young women: "You don't have to have a family to be happy or to feel successful or fulfilled. You don't have to have a family."

Kallie Marie: Great. And do you think that this is different for men with regard to being limited? Is it easier for men to have a family in the studio than it is for women?

Sylvia Massy: Yes, because of the nature—because of the dynamics between men and women. Women are more likely to be in a supporting role than men. I think that it's very difficult for men to be in a supporting role. Just for the nature of who they are, we are. So it is much easier, I think, for men to continue with their career and have a supporting spouse or partner who will take care of those things at home, or the children or whatever, and keep track of them. So, yeah, there is a difference there as far as families go. Big difference between men and women being able to continue with their career.

Kallie Marie: How do you think we could make things more balanced to change that? Or is this part of a larger societal thing that will just have to wait because—

Sylvia Massy: It is, and I don't think that there's anything wrong with that. It's at the core of our—and I hate to say it—animal, but it's an animal thing, where men are the breadwinners and they keep things secure and the women take care of other things in the household and basically cared for more. Men don't want to be cared for by women, not necessarily. So it's just a human dynamic, I think, that if—I am not even sure what the answer would be to that. How could it be easier for women? It would have to be that the men would accept a supporting role in life more often and be able to make less money [than] their spouse or their partner. This is a big issue for men. I can't blame them for . . . having this need to be the head of the household. So here's one way that it would have worked for me, is if my husband had been independently wealthy and didn't have to worry about money at all and then I could just—we could have a housekeeper and a nanny. But, you know, that's unrealistic for most people. That's the only solution that I could think of at this point anyway. Maybe we will evolve to be more balanced in the future. But we are still men and we are still women.

Johnette Napolitano: "A family is death to an artist"—Woody Allen.

Kerry Pompeo: Well, the notion of me having children is I don't want them, so I've never really, like, had that in my head. I know that my studio and my work is my child that I nurture. That said, I do like to make it a point. I do feel like it's kind of like I want to present that to people or put that on the table, that I don't want kids, because people would then think, "Oh, is she gonna take a year off?"—you know? But, hey, what if I just want to take a year off because of *me*, you know? But I don't want kids. But that being said, children, I think, are really important. I still, like, have a real connection with young girls coming up in the business, which is why I do things like The Girls' Club and other, like, youth groups and work with Sesame Street, and I think that that is very important to try to keep that in mind.

> **Kallie Marie:** How do you feel that this is different for men? The reason I am asking is because I am aware that there are plenty of men that work in the recording industry that have children, and yet for us [women] it is different. The point of this question is, How can we make this more balanced and how is it different for men? Because once we highlight how it is different for men, we may see answers emerge for how we can make things balanced for women who do want kids or for people for it to be a nonissue so we don't have to go around making it known—

Kerry Pompeo: I think that men should be able to get paternity leave too. Like, my best friend just had a baby, you know, a couple of years ago now, but time flies. You know, it's just as important for a dad to be able to be with their child as a mom is. Then they're like, "But they're not going to be around as much" or "They're not going to be as attentive." But I don't know why that is such a stigma that is surrounding women. Because, why wouldn't a man be attentive to his kid? I don't know—I don't have the answer to that! You know, I've never really given it thought. I just know I don't want 'em. God, I was a crazy child, so it would probably come back to me tenfold. Maybe, you know what? It's funny that I always say that if I was old and bored, I would adopt. My dad was adopted so . . . You know, that's why, like, I'm not on a time clock. So—but I feel for women who are! Because that's gotta suck to have to make a career choice or for it to even—for them to even have to weigh that option or for them—or for other people to view them—

    Kallie Marie: —through that lens—

Kerry Pompeo: Yeah! Like, are people viewing me like that? When I am applying for a job? Absolutely! But then, I've never really given it thought. There are definitely walls that need to come down around that.

Ebonie Smith: I'm a little different from a lot of women, that I never really had that deep longing for kids. I never—I'm just starting to think about it in my early thirties, and just like literally just now. I'm kind of in a position of where I wonder how it will work, because so much time in the studio, like, an unbelievable amount of time, and I don't really know where I would fit a kid. I don't know where I would fit a partner, you know? And the women that I see doing it, I've seen female producers and women engineers who have made it work, and it's not without sacrifice. But I've seen them make it work.

One of the things I think about men is a lot of my male peers are almost all married, and all of them, almost all of them, are married and have wives and girlfriends and kids, and they just don't miss a beat; it just is what it is. You know, I was in the studio with a major artist once for twenty-four hours straight, and I think I was one of two women. The other woman was a manager, and I was the only woman in the technical position. There was probably twenty people in the studio between, like, band members, producers, and engineers; it was a really robust session. And why I remember? One of the guys getting the phone call from a girlfriend or wife, you know, in the middle of the night, and him being like, "Look, you know what it is. You know how this goes," like, "Don't call me with this," like, "You know I am in the studio; you know this is how this goes." Once the morning hit, got around eight, then he finally said, "You know, we have been here twenty-four hours; I have to go get my kids from school. I have to go over, take my kids to school." So I remember thinking to myself, like, "How many men would be on the other side of that phone call?" Like, or, "How many partners of women would be on the other side of that phone call?" Like, "You know what it is. I am in the studio. You know how this goes." Like, how many men or women who are dating women would be cool with that?

So, I just—for me, I haven't dated that much because I'm always in the studio. I feel like I'm always there, and I think that's the sacrifice that I make. I think that women, a lot of times, that men there, my male peers and their partners can sometimes be maybe a little bit more . . . *supportive* is not the word, but more flexible with the men, do their type of thing, staying out all hours and not come home, working twenty-four hours and taking off months at a time, on a world tour, with somebody, or producing a record halfway across the country. I think the girlfriends and the wives can, I think—are a little more accepting. Maybe it's because the money is there. Like, if your man has the job half across the world but, you know, he's bringing home real money, then maybe that's more accepting to some wives and some girlfriends.

I don't really know. I thought about it, because it seems like it's taking everything just for me to get in this position, and I haven't really felt like I could sacrifice the time to cultivate romance and relationships. But that's on me. I don't think that every woman feels that way or that every female producer feels that way. Gender Amplified just did a great interview with Georgia Anne [Muldrow], and she just had a baby. She's an incredible producer, and she's married, and she's extremely successful as a producer. I think it's more me than the landscape. There are lots of women that do this with kids, so I don't know. I can't really speak to it as a whole, but I can speak to it as my experience.

Kallie Marie: Have people made any assumptions with regard to this notion of kids or relationships in terms of your career?

Ebonie Smith: I don't know what people assume. I would imagine that people assume that I don't have kids, and that assumption would be right. I don't know if they think I don't want kids. Like, nobody's ever really voiced anything that I've, like, you know, heard. I would imagine that people assume that I don't want to have kids because I spend a lot of time in the studio. There is a female executive in the office, though, that I assumed didn't have kids. I was like, there's no way this woman has [kids]; she works, like, constantly. And she has, like, three kids! And a super supportive husband, you know? So, I don't know. There are some executives, more than one in the office, and I just assumed they didn't have them because it's just so workaholic about everything; I just assumed they didn't. But then when I find out they have kids and they are married, I was like, "Whoa! Who's with these children?" That's me, being a bit of an asshole, because I have the same stereotypes going through my mind of a woman: if a woman has kids, then she should probably be with them. Which is probably the stereotype, right? That clearly you can't leave the kids with a man—oh my god, like, who is raising these kids?? Oh, right—the kids are going to turn out crazy!

Kallie Marie: [Laughs] Right, like men are not adults too?

Ebonie Smith: Right! Like, oh god, so, I definitely have made my own assumptions, but I don't know in general about me, what people assume, because people come in the studio, they work, they leave.

Kallie Marie: Last on this topic: How is this different for men in the studio, having children, and how can we make things more balanced, if you think it needs to be more balanced?

Ebonie Smith: Oh, that's tough. I guess the obvious answer is at-work day care. I always think it's super progressive when organizations do that type of thing. I know it's very rare, and it's a liability for a lot of companies, so I don't know if that will be a real solution, a realistic solution. Also, twenty-four-hour day-care services. I think, in general, we can just all become a little bit more open-minded about who can care for kids. I am pretty traditional in my perspective, because I didn't grow up with a father, so I was raised by my mother and her mother and my great-grandmother. So I just kind of think children should be with moms. But that's because of my upbringing. Let me just say, like, if I were to have kids, I would want to be there a lot. You know what I mean? I would never want to put that responsibility off on my husband or wife or whatever. I would want to be there as much as I could be.

Andrea Yankovsky: That did [affect me], and I also delayed it—a lot of women do—because you['d] be more established in your field. Whatever field that is, not just this industry. So, on a couple levels, you are making choices about your career if you want to have kids. I mean, some women are just okay not to. I think I knew I wanted to have kids eventually, so, yeah, that factored into my longer-term planning and the decisions that I was making.

Kallie Marie: Have people made any assumptions with regard to yourself, about kids during your career? Or do you have any experiences where people assumed things about what you could or couldn't do based on that?

Andrea Yankovsky: I don't think so. Again, I think maybe I haven't experienced that quite so much. It was just because a lot of the men I was working with were having kids at the time.

Kallie Marie: How is this different for men?

Andrea Yankovsky: Oh, it's totally different. [Laughs] Some of it is just the logistics of—I mean, for example, you're the one who is pregnant, or what if you have a difficult pregnancy? What if you are struck by morning sickness and you are having issues or whatever? It's tough. And then in terms of—I don't know where to start on this, because it's different, it really is. And even when my husband's really, I would say he's pretty enlightened, but at the same time it's like, he's still a guy. [Laughs]

Kallie Marie: Right—he's still raised in the culture that we are in, so it's hard to remove everything. Well, with regard to children, how can we make things more balanced in the studio for people having families, men or women, but women especially who want to continue being producers?

Andrea Yankovsky: That's tough . . . That's a really good question, because I think it's—there's things that people can do on a personal level, but there's also things that just . . . I experienced this when I had—this is really funny. My kids were born early. My husband was at work when my water broke, and I had to get to the hospital. He kept working because we just didn't know what was going on. It was early, and so there was really no reason for him to be at the hospital; it wasn't like I needed [him], and they were going to transfer me, so it was like, I knew where I was going to be, so he just stayed at work! I was cool with that. But by virtue of the fact I was being transferred in labor, you know, he kept on working, and then the next day when they were born, he took the day off, he was in there, and all that sort of stuff. The day after that, I think he slept. But after that, he didn't have to take any time off, and this is an interesting thing, and I don't know how much this affects people with full-term babies, because, again, I just had a different experience. So, my kids stayed in the ICU for a while because they were early, so we didn't have to bring babies home right away. So, effectively, he didn't have to take any family leave because I was the one that had to go to the hospital every day and deliver the milk and all of that, and he kept on working. Because also, while he doesn't have his own business, the fact that he is working at a job that doesn't have paid paternity leave, that's a big deal, so he needed to keep on working, because I wasn't working. You know, that's sort of the financial reality. So the whole childcare role stuff fell on me. So, for the whole time that they were in the hospital, he could come after work, but he was the one that was still working. I even remember, in the studios, when engineers were having kids, you know, they would be out for a couple days, and then they would be back at work. And that's awesome that they can do that!

Whether or not they are able to make that choice—again, due to personal preferences, financial considerations, all that sort of stuff— but also, just, their bodies didn't just give birth. They can just be right back at it, no problemo, and frankly that is something that I was not prepared for was the whole postpartum period! Holy shit! Your body's been through hell, and I was wanting to go back to work at that point. So, you know, even putting together blanket policy for something like that . . . and I think that another thing is that, honestly, and I am guilty of it too, is that, now that I have kids, I think I am also much more empathetic and more understanding of women that have kids. Sort of going back to the—sometimes women are worse to other women, I think my attitude toward women with kids now is a lot different now that I've had this experience and realized, firsthand, how exhausting it is and how much energy you put into it and what a huge life change it is and all that sort of stuff. I think as a result, in terms of working with women, you know, that are doing that sort of stuff, it's a big deal. And, you know, God, I keep going back to the fact that I put off having kids; some people have fertility issues. And that is both a biological component, an economic component, an emotional component too . . . and for the most part I still have to deal with that.

> **Kallie Marie:** Do you think that keeps women out of music production, or do you think it just makes it different in a way? My focus in asking these questions is to raise awareness so that hopefully we can see some changes around women in the workplace. I know everybody is fighting [in the United States] for maternity and paternity leave. The music industry is really such an odd business that that's not going to be the case or possible to work for everybody . . .

Andrea Yankovsky: I completely agree. I think we have so many freelancers, right? So we are not working with traditional workplace policies or relaying big brother legislation or health care. Do you even have health insurance? That was a huge issue for a while. So, it's a really big deal. I think a lot more awareness, . . . but the problem is—and I think sometimes it seems like at the end of the day if people want to be really kind and compassionate, they still have to go about their business. If you are not available because of XYZ or your schedule becomes unreliable, people factor that in because they still have to get their job done. So if you're having childcare issues or, say, you are pregnant and having health issues and you can't engineer a session or something like that, they're not . . . sometimes if you have a loyal client or whatever they will reschedule, but sometimes people have a deadline, and they just need to get their shit done.

It's such an individual thing, too; depends on who your partner is and what their beliefs and assumptions are. Or another issue is women having children without partners. I know a few women who have done that—that have adopted or gotten donors or ended up single and it wasn't their plan, or they are divorced or widowed, all that sort of stuff. And that's the single-parent phenomenon too.

Anonymous: This has not affected me much. I don't have kids, but when I think of having them in the future, it reminds me of the challenges of having a career that is very freelance-driven and in which it's very rare to get benefits through your job. So the main issue is that most engineers and producers work freelance, and in the US without socialized medicine and maternity leave it is very difficult and stressful to work as an independent contractor.

I never felt like I was discriminated for the possibility of getting pregnant, and I don't feel any assumptions have been made around it.

However, in some of my experience, I have noticed that men with children have received better treatment at work—more or longer shifts, benefits, laxness with regards to punctuality, accommodation with scheduling, et cetera—justified by the fact that they have children. Perhaps women with children would get the same treatment; I have nothing to compare it to. But I would doubt it, since women are not seen as "breadwinners" the way men are. Most women in production I know do not have kids.

MICROAGGRESSIONS AND SOFT SEXISM: IS THE OUTCOME CAREER FATIGUE?
Microaggressions and soft sexism may be more common than overt sexism, which are more often difficult to spot and/or handle. How do you think this factors into career fatigue for women in music production? How have you dealt with these types of challenges and sidestepped this kind of career fatigue?

Abhita Austin: I definitely went through career fatigue. Its huge. I have seen—and I am thinking back to when I was coming up in the studio system—even seeing the interns, who would come through the door, get burned out. I can imagine it was exhausting, and it was exhausting for me, but I kept moving forward. But I can remember, at one point, I was not engineering. I stopped. Because it was just *a lot*. To me it's beyond; it felt like it was even beyond being woman, and it's just the hours, the pay—it was not great. It's just many different factors. Its management; a lot of times they are A-holes. You would think that they would be on your team, but they always take the side of the client. So there's no loyalty in that way.

Kallie Marie: So that's an experience for everybody, regardless of gender?

Abhita Austin: Yeah, I'm thinking. Is it different 'cause I am a woman? Is it different in particular because I am a Black woman? Maybe! I don't know, because all the higher-ups were White men. So I don't know. But I knew that it was exhausting, and it felt like my soul was being killed. So I am always very sensitive to that. I just stepped away. This was, like, the mid-2000s? I just stepped away. Then I rebranded and started working on a studio in Long Island, which was smaller—still great board, great equipment, so still on a great level. But there I started from the ground up again because I couldn't come in as an assistant.

I had to go backwards, and kind of, like, settle or whatever—figure out what I wanted to do. I had to go backwards to go forwards.

Kallie Marie: How have you dealt with these kinds of challenges and sidestepped the career fatigue?

Abhita Austin: I don't know if I sidestepped it. I think that it had a lot to do with my trajectory because in a way I just kind of—that made me go in a more independent route, because it just felt like death almost, like a spiritual death. The amount of stuff you had to fight against, and to me the overall—I got a sense of the overall feeling that you were always being thought of as less-than. I feel like that's not natural, and, again, I was younger; all the stuff you are processing, you are trying to figure yourself out, but that's what it felt like. I think whether or not we believe it . . . we're not that. There's a light and a greatness within us, so if you are perceiving this—What is this? There was just a conflict there, and I was like, "You know what? I am going to put this down for a minute." So I felt like if I would have kept on pushing in that direction, maybe I will have some plaques under my belt or whatever, but I did not, you know what I mean? And I feel like I am spiritually better for it.

> **Kallie Marie:** Well, you have to take care of yourself at the end of the day. Could you elaborate a little bit on how the microaggressions were fatiguing for you or what kinds of microaggressions you experienced? Or were you saying, as you mentioned earlier, it was just an overarching feeling?

Abhita Austin: It was a lot of second-guessing. It was kind of like, it's almost like you're as good as your last gig type of thing. Like I said, I felt like there was little support. The pay was not great, for starters; you're trying to live, and then there was little support in a sense where, and I am thinking, just from the gatekeepers, the management, the people that are paying you. There's little confidence, they are saying it verbally, but this is where the micro[aggression] comes in, where the actions are not reflecting what they are saying. So, it's just like, "What's going on?" If anything, I know the client is always right, but a lot of these folks are crazy or like on something in the session. So I guess that's passive-aggressive? Although it's being said, there is no confidence and loyalty to you as somebody who is putting work into a company. To me that was draining.

> **Kallie Marie:** Okay, maybe that's an experience that is surely shared by men as well?

Abhita Austin: It could be, yeah.

Leslie M. G. Bird: See, microaggressions are very possible. For example, if a client walks in and assumes you're not the engineer and looks at the male in the room for guidance, it's almost like right then you have a feeling of not being respected, and that has happened to me. I think right away if there's a technical problem that comes up, as they always do, and you're scrambling to figure it out, I have . . . even [heard] other women say, "Can you get someone to help you?" It's like, well, if a guy was having the problem, I wonder if it was a male, if they would have more patience like, "Oh, I'm sure this is a really complex problem he needs to figure it out."

It's usually shoptalk and I think we could point to as something that seemingly puts women at a disadvantage when it doesn't. So for example, "Have you heard of the latest ZX 1000? How could you not know about the latest ZX 1000?? Well, how could you not know about it? You must not know what you're doing!" Those are the kinds of things that drive me nuts. So, yeah, I hate that stuff. I don't have anybody who's going to say, "You don't know what you're doing, woman." Fortunately I don't know any man that's going to be that much of a . . . I don't think any of the stuff we have to deal with—because, you know, fortunately no man is idiot enough to say something so overtly sexist. So it's almost like any sexism we face is going to be this underhanded stuff.

> **Kallie Marie:** Do you think that this is a factor in career fatigue for yourself or for other women? How have you dealt with these challenges and sidestepped this kind of career fatigue?

Leslie M. G. Bird: I do. I think it's important to have a network of women to talk to, and I think having the opportunity to share your frustrations with people of the same gender rather than having things mansplained to you—because when I personally, you know, talking in sort of Facebook groups or whatever, when guys get in there, "I don't want to hear your perspective, thank you!" I don't want to hear from him, and we're not going through the same thing. As for me and that world, I would answer, to take yourself out of email and come back into and just know, "I'm awesome! Get back to the studio, and get back to being great."

Hillary Johnson: Okay, I've never heard that term. I like that actually: *career fatigue*. You know, again, I think that we are in a time where what you're talking about is probably all there is. In other words, there's no blatant sexism. It's all subtle. Unless [it's] just really obnoxious and you're like, "This is ridiculous. Get the hell out of here!" But I mean, again, when I started, I keep referring back to when I started, because when you start that's when you get all your confidence and experience, and [if] you don't have those two things, then you're gonna have career fatigue really quickly. I think if you have confidence and experience, because any sexism is sort of like, well, it's, like, just par for the course. You either ignore it or you address it and you move on. I don't really think it's fatiguing, except for maybe certain unique situations. And in that case, just that person is fatiguing. Like anything, you go to the grocery store and you have to deal with the same cashier who is fatiguing, and [you're] just like, "Oh, whatever—[I've] got to go to the store and deal with that guy!" Whatever.

> **Kallie Marie:** Have you dealt with these types of challenges at all in either career fatigue or microaggressions?

Hillary Johnson: Oh, sure! Well, career fatigue in that sense, no. But career fatigue in the sense that I am working twelve-hour days for many days in a row? Yes. But you know, in that sense, how much longer can I do this? I really—I think if I did the same exact job every day, five days a week, six days a week, forever? Then I would have career fatigue. But because I do so much different stuff, all related to what I like—I record bands, I do live sound, I master records, I work in company designing audio visual systems, I am technician at a studio,

I kind of bounce around a lot—and that keeps me from getting career fatigue. But the sexism and the microaggression, I just ignore it. I guess I am just so used to it, and, you know, again, when I started out it was so different. It wasn't—things were becoming politically correct, so men were sort of learning how to be, and now they know how to be, and they either choose to subscribe to it or not. So it's easier now, I guess. Women have it easy now.

Kallie Marie: Do you feel like microaggressions have just dropped off? Is that what you are saying?

Hillary Johnson: I dunno that it dropped off. I think it's just that maybe I don't notice it as much because it's part of the life, part of the gig, part of being a person on the planet, really. You deal with it in personal life; you deal with it in your work life; it's just part of being a woman. Yeah, I don't think that's going to change with any other kind of global change or societal change. I don't think that will translate. I think that anything that happens out in the world or in our immediate society just sort of trickles down into the studio. I don't think that only the studio will change.

Sylvia Massy: No. You know, maybe I am beyond this kind of dance between sexes in the studio where, you know, people are playing different roles. I think I am beyond that, because pretty much if someone hires me to work on their music, they are very interested in what I have to say. They're not pushing me one way or another or giving me any kind of subtle hints . . . that I need to play a certain role as a woman. We are just musician and producer. Sexes don't matter at that point. I'm very fortunate to be beyond that now. It may be that there's things in the studio [that] happen between men and women when the women are starting out that they may find difficult to deal with, but I suggest that those things will go away. You do have to prove yourself as being able to do the job, and that goes with anyone who is starting out. But maybe those kinds of subtle gestures feel a little colder and meaner when you're a woman. Maybe.

Johnette Napolitano: I'm not really familiar enough with these new type terms. Just the language speaks to me of more school than experience. Wanna produce? Own your own studio. Burnout happens to everyone. I sew a few hours a day, keep balance, study languages. You can't be interesting or equipped to deal with people on any level if you're not rounded out as a person yourself.

Kerry Pompeo: You know, things like, "Do you want me to get that for you so that you don't break a nail?" It's always something like that. Like, "No, if I was worried about my nails, like, I would have a desk job," right? And those are, like, little things, and it's like, yeah, I do have those moments where it's just like, "Oh, come on, dude." But, you know . . . to be honest, no. I would just say it's life in general, that dudes just say some dumb things. So, you know, for it to be, like, work specific? Maybe it's just life specific?

Ebonie Smith: Oh, no, it's exhausting. Microaggressions are exhausting for everybody. Men, women, children, dogs. . . . Everybody that can't be direct annoys me. It makes me feel like the odd fish out because I am so direct. I just—because I can, like, have assertiveness and confidence. Some of the more annoying microaggressions, the ones I am most annoyed by—so, looking like you can't lift anything or push anything or have ten thousand guys try to, you know, move a box that looks heavy but doesn't have anything in it. "It just looks like you shouldn't be carrying this. Do you need some help?" You know? That can be exhausting for a woman engineer or producer, because it definitely does translate as you not being able to do your job. If your job calls for you to move gear, then let me do my job. If I need some help, I will ask for it. It's a difference if I'm going to the airport and I have a heavy bag and I need you and you want to be chivalrous. But this is my job; this is something I get paid for. So if I need some assistance, the most important thing would be [for me] to ask for it. But this is part of my job description, to move gear, so I can move it. You know what I mean? That's something I don't think that the guys just are just going to have to . . . I can understand it is difficult for them, because they've been taught to be respectful men, and it is respectful to help a woman with something heavy—it is. But the thing that gets complicated in this, this is not just helping a woman with something heavy; this is trying to do a woman's job. It's a difference, you know? It's that subtle difference that men have not been trained to deal with. There's no training to deal with it, so that's number one.

Another microaggression is a gender thing and a race thing, which is the inability to relate to somebody that is different or assuming, oh gosh, it is such an issue that I can't even articulate it right. It's [this] thing of not wanting to be—not wanting to, with women and with race, its thing of not wanting to be offending to [the] person with less privilege. [Which] ends up not being honest and not being transparent. Because there's a struggle with the need to be politically correct, so you don't want to say something rude to a woman, or you don't want [to say] something rude to a Black person, or you don't want to say something rude to a poor person, so you don't tell the truth, and that is annoying. Just be direct! Like, I don't need you to soften the blow; just tell the truth, and let me deal with it. It's not offensive if it's the truth. You know, if it's true, it's not offensive. So I think there's an issue with political correctness that keeps people from being direct, as direct as they need to be, with people they perceive . . . as having less privilege.

The last one is the assumption of a lack of competence in areas, which can come across in a passive aggressive way. An example would be assuming that you know that I don't know how to use certain tools or assuming that I can't learn. I think the thing that is most frustrating is not being given an assignment because there's a fear that I don't know how to do it. You know, I probably don't know how to do it, but I'm super smart, though; you can still give me the assignment, and I will figure out how to do it. Trust that I can learn! That's something that is frustrating too, as a microaggression. Like, the assumption that you can't learn something.

> **Kallie Marie:** That creates an entry barrier! Because people can't trust and won't take a chance letting someone learn something or believing that you can do it, and so then you never get to do it, and then you quote, unquote, "don't have any experience," so then it's this big cycle of not trusting and not believing and then not getting to do it, and before you know it, people ask, "What have you done?" And you're like, "Well, nothing, but give me a chance!" and the response is, "Well, no, because you haven't done anything." I know that entry barriers exist for everybody in lots of fields and for male and female, but I think that there is a specific thing around being a woman with technology where people are like, "Nahhhhhhh . . . this is really technical; this might be too technical for you."

Ebonie Smith: I say all the time, I just want the privilege of being able to fail. I learn more from failing than anything else, and I would like the privilege to fail. I think there is this pervasive need or desire to keep women from failing. You know, we don't—generally, in society, men want to be able to rescue or solve problems for women. "You don't have to fail, because I can just do it for you." Or "You don't have to fail, because I can just solve the problem." It's kind of like, "No, I want to be the best human being I can be, so let me fail. Let me fail, especially if it's something that is not life or death," you know what I mean? And failing at putting something together or failing at doing something technical—if it's not the end all be all, then it's okay! Because, with my interns, I train them, I give them a real good briefing, but I like for them to fail. I like to throw them into stuff, like, if it's a no-pressure situation. If there's a big artist in the studio, I can't afford it; but, you know, I have to just do things. But when we have slow days, I will throw them into a lot of scenarios just to know what I need to teach them, and a lot of times they will do lots of things wrong and that lets me know, "Okay, good." It also lets me know the type of personality I am dealing with, because some people will do something wrong before they will ask for help. So I need to know that about a person; I need to know their personality traits, and I need to know the type of people I am working with and managing. So I will kind of just throw people in a situation ,and they will just kind of do something wrong, and I will go, "All you had to do was ask for help." . . . I know that type of worker I have, and I always love the type of interns that I will give an assignment to, who will go, "I don't know how to do this." That lets me know that that's somebody I can really trust when it's crunch time. And it teaches me too; it teaches me to be the type of person to ask for help, because that's how you learn, how you get better. You have to put people in scenarios where they make good decisions. Giving them the option to fail teaches them a lot about who they are and lets you know about who they are as an employer or as manager or whoever.

Kallie Marie: Do you have any tactics that you use to help you deal with sidestepping career fatigue, whether it's because of microaggressions or just in general? Because audio engineering and producing, the whole industry, can be career fatiguing. What sort of tactics do you use to deal with both?

Ebonie Smith: Well, there's for me, as a Christian, there's prayer and meditation, and there's stepping outside of the industry drama and fatigue to make sure I am reading the Bible and going to church and making sure that I am taking some time every day to make an account of the things that I am grateful for. Eating right—food, it's so critical. Bringing your food, making sure you are getting tons of water when you are doing these long sessions that were only supposed to be two hours that end up being eight hours, like, all that type of thing. Like, bringing your food is so critical, making sure you have a good balance, working out. I like to work out; it helps me with fatigue. Just staying fit helps me with fatigue, tons of water. Another thing is counsel: you've got to have people in life who serve as advisors and counselors. I really do think that if you are doing production or engineering, you should try to keep a therapist or somebody, because people unload on you a lot. They unload on you because they are trying to facilitate help; they're trying to facilitate creative process with themselves. There's a lot of unloading that they do. Dealing with different temperaments, you have to be grounded yourself, and it's hard to be grounded yourself if you have all these things that you need to unload on someone. So, a therapist, somebody you see once a month at the minimum, is really good, especially when you are dealing with industry politics and other things, career planning. If you are engineer or producer, you definitely have to always be on your feet in terms of hustling and jobs; you can never really get comfortable. So you want somebody in your life that helps you strategize, to be introspective, to kind of come outside of the grind of music making to think about who you are, who you wanna be, and the proper plan for that, accordingly, to have a professional plan with, but also with the perspective of mental health. That's critical, to stay grounded, and just making sure that you are having fun. Whatever you do to have fun, do it. At least give yourself some time every week—if it's Netflix, going to the park, you know, making self-time. It's very easy to get stuck in the studio working on a record for a month and never see sun. It's really easy, so you don't wanna crack up, man. You wanna be good. So many producers are half crazy. From the drugs and just being in the studio with no sunlight, there's a lot of crazy-ass producers out there! You know, you don't want to be a nut job. You want to be solid, because you are taking steps to be in this game for a long time. Think about all the people that fizz out. They have a couple good years, and they fizz—they go crazy, they start doing drugs. I don't really wanna be—I don't care enough about the industry to do that to myself. The only reason I tolerate the music industry is I love making music, and this is still, like, the only game in town if you want to be a professional and you want to make good money at it. The industry is the only game in town, as far as just trying to be in it. Like, I am in it because I want to make records. So I am not going to let it drive me crazy.

Andrea Yankovsky: I'll bet you—I mean, I have a background in social psychology and cognitive neuroscience, and I will bet you anything that, if we even look at—if some sort of imperial research were done, that it has an effect, whether we know it or not. It's that same part of fatigue of that.

Kallie Marie: Because of the extra cognitive load?

Andrea Yankovsky: Exactly. Whether it bothers them or not, it doesn't matter—it's there. It's like the kids at the school are in the flight path of the airport; they learn how to tune it out but still has an effect. I would generally just ignore it, but I feel like it also . . . Yeah, just ignore it. That was my coping mechanism. Just don't show, and even if it bothers you, don't let them—don't show it; don't let them see that it bothers you. Because then they are just going to do it more.

Kallie Marie: Does it impact our output? Does it impact our functioning as we are working? And how do we cope with that, because, for the foreseeable [future], it's not going anywhere. We can ignore it, but there is still a level of processing that's going on that has to be impacting my cognitive ability as I am making technical decisions or dealing with a piece of gear that's not working properly or fielding a bunch of things at once. And, again, this will be different for everyone.

Andrea Yankovsky: Right. I mean, we still don't have an equal rights amendment. I mean, there's such a cognitive cost to having to switch your focus and attention . . . whether you know it or not, it's a fact. I think early [in] my career so much of the expectation was just to disappear. And the funny thing is, is that, I guess, I think that's easier for women to do. So that, whether that's how you dress or how you act, but then you're expected—it's funny in the music industry when you are sort of coming up and paying your dues, you're expected to disappear, and there's also a little bit of an undercurrent of, I wouldn't call it subservience, but there's such a hierarchy, and I feel like often there was a, how would you say, this mentality of, not making it better or easier or more comfortable for the next—for the people coming up underneath you; not me per se, but whether it was another engineer, there was more of a mentality, of well, you know, "I had to do it." I understand people's reaction to [a] sense of entitlement, or people who kind of, I wouldn't say, don't know their place but don't understand the culture or the how-to of their role in the process. But there is such a huge leap from—especially now, because, really, the highest role in a studio is an assistant as engineer. Sometimes there's the staff engineer; there's chief engineer. But most of the time it's engineers, and producers are coming in from the outside. So . . . so, that was something that I remember facing, going, "Holy shit—how do I do this?" because it used to be that there were staff engineer positions and that the engineers that were engineering the sessions were confident of their job security, right? So they could afford to walk out of the session and let the assistant engineer the rest of it. They could afford to even not show up. And they could also afford to give people more credit. But now, there was a time when, again, we are talking about scarcer resources, when engineers, I mean, god, like, I am thinking early in the, like, 2000s. I remember there were so many top engineers and Grammy-winning, multiplatinum, amazing engineers that were not working. Okay, if they're not getting business, then I remember, again, trying to make the shift from assistant to regular engineer, it's like, "Oh my god, how am I going to do this?" and also the mentality of, "Okay, I go from being invisible to all of a sudden having to be confident and promote myself in a way that I am comfortable with and be the person that's running the session, have all eyes on me when shit goes down." [Laughs] That's a big jump for anybody. I think when you are women it's probably harder.

> **Kallie Marie:** Do you have any ideas why you think it might be harder? Or do you care to comment? In my estimation, I want to be careful about just saying things are harder without quantifying why.

Andrea Yankovsky: That's just sort of my gut feeling. So, as an assistant, again, you're expected to be completely transparent. It's like you're wallpaper: you're expected to not exist, and your job needs to be—it just needs to happen, and you shouldn't be seen or heard. I think women are good at doing that. And then . . . but in terms of how it is, I think for men it's, if you are confident, it's more socially acceptable for men to brag. And if they're going—and if women are already the quote, unquote, "good assistants," they are already leaning toward being more of the invisible, having to go make a larger leap . . .

> **Kallie Marie:** I wonder if also, if you're the assistant, it's kind of like someone has already vouched for your technical prowess, by the fact that you are there. But if you're trying to sell yourself as a producer or head engineer, flying solo, you're having to convince people of your technical prowess. That's not an assumed part of feminine identity, I would say . . .

Andrea Yankovsky: Yeah, sort of imposter syndrome or feeling like a fraud. Like, "How did I convince these people to let me engineer their record? If they only knew." We do that, and, I mean, all people do that, of course, but we do that despite the facts. I remember, just looking at my personality, and what I do, I've always been kind of a high achiever, not because it was about achievement but because it was about pushing myself to what I am capable of and realizing your potential. Different people have different potential in different areas, right? So, especially in an area that I am passionate about, or sometimes it doesn't even matter if I am good at it, if I just like it, I get enjoyment from seeing, from gaining mastery at something or sort of fulfilling my promise. That can translate into high achievement in a lot of areas. And so, even when I was in audio school in the conservatory, I was at the top of my class, not because I was concerned but because that's how it works, because I was, "Oh, this is really cool," and I just did it and went with it. So, I think that I took the technical competence; you gain confidence. So I would often root myself in being damn good at what I did. So, whether it was being a damn good assistant, whether it was figuring out the console that just got installed, because I am also so curious, sometimes intellectually curious, sometimes I need to be saved from my own self.

I like to think outside the box and find solutions to problems that are really challenging. But I think what can often happen is—one of my least favorite words in the entire English language is *overachiever*. Because it implies excess, too much, in a bad way. It's one thing to say *high*, but it's another thing to say *over*. Also the emphasis is on achievement as opposed to just fulfillment. So, where I am going with this is that was one of my—that was one of the ways that I managed myself in the industry, because I could always fall back on being good at what I did. And a lot of women will say, "Oh, we have to be better." I don't [know] whether or not that is true, in terms of my own personal experience, but I just come at things from saying, "Okay, I am going to be good at this." The flip side of that is that sometimes you stall out because you don't feel like you are good enough, or you wait because you think that, like, "Oh, I'm going to wait until this is perfect," or "I am going to wait to do this until, you know, I feel confident to do it." Instead of just jumping in and doing it.

Anonymous: It is definitely exhausting to challenge stereotypes and be reminded of your gender on a daily basis. It is also difficult to talk about [it] with male coworkers, because they likely [don't] see it or don't think it's an issue. So, although it's good to speak up about it, I try to find more productive and meaningful ways of venting my frustration about it. Because trying to convince people of something you know you're experiencing and [then] being denied your experiences or made light of them only adds more weight and exhaustion.

I try not to let it get me down by reminding myself of the awesome people who have been supportive, helpful, and professional with me. I stopped publicly complaining about every daily sexist microaggression, and instead when I feel frustrated or have a weird experience, I write it out in a journal or put it into song lyrics. I also take time to remind myself of male coworkers and friends who have helped me on my journey, because I think it's really important not to forget them. I also like to give people the benefit of the doubt, and if someone disrespects me, I imagine they have their own issues they're dealing with and it's not always personal.

I think if you don't focus on the negative, it doesn't weigh you down so much. The important part is staying in the career, because just a woman's presence alone in that job is creating a shift and chipping away at the patriarchal paradigm.

3

THE IMPORTANCE AND IMPACT OF WOMEN IN MUSIC PRODUCTION AND AUDIO ENGINEERING

Music is a diverse landscape with people of all kinds, globally participating, creating, and sharing in its exploration and enjoyment. It is only natural that all parts of society have the potential and possibility to contribute to their society's music in any way they choose to. Creating a landscape that reflects this diversity not only promotes but also encourages growth, participation, and engagement. For many, asking "Why diversity, and why now?" is a no-brainer but often difficult to articulate, especially in the face of a detractor. This section focuses on finding out from the women in the field the why and how as they see it and how they themselves, with all their collective experiences and knowledge, would choose to express their thoughts on this topic.

The goal is to be inclusive and not to have "women's music," like "women's art," as somehow separate and not quite equal to the rest of music being made. Rather than othering the underrepresented, inclusive endeavors should encourage diversity and foster visibility. Visibility and mentorship are key components of the impact and importance of having more marginalized groups in any space. Visibility is its own indirect mentorship in a way. Representation signals to those around them that participating and achieving is possible, and in turn people can mentally envision taking part in these activities themselves. It also normalizes participation of otherwise underrepresented groups and helps dismantle deeply ingrained cultural assumptions about stereotypical roles in society. These are visible role models. And for many years, prior to the current visibility that the Internet has brought, most women will have operated without them.

With increased visibility there will hopefully be a reduction in stereotype threat. Representation and visibility are strong counters to stereotype threat—something that can be experienced by any marginalized group in any setting. So, for example, if men are the marginalized group—say, as nurses or preschool teachers—they might experience stereotype threat, too. A stereotype is incredibly complex both in how it affects a person's working memory and performance of a complex task and also in how it affects their promotion focus and switches the brain into a mode of protection and caution or, rather, makes people less confident as they fear failure. (We discuss confidence and comfort with technology in the next section of the book, and knowing that the two are linked also provides even further insights to the types of challenges that people in these situations face.)

Psychologist Cordelia Fine explains stereotype threat and its effects:

Although you might think that suppressing negative stereotypical thoughts would help women, it doesn't. [Psychologist Christine] Logel found that the more women suppressed irrational woman concepts, the worse they performed. The reason for this seems to be because suppressing unwanted thoughts and anxieties uses up mental resources that could be put to better use elsewhere. To perform well in a demanding mental task you have to remain focused. This involves keeping accessible the information you need for your computations, as well as keeping out of consciousness anything that is irrelevant or distracting. This mental housekeeping is the duty of what is known as working memory or executive control. Most people facing a difficult and important intellectual challenge are likely to have a few intrusive self-doubts and anxieties. But as we've seen, people performing under stereotype threat have more. This places an extra load on working memory—to the detriment of the cognitive feat you are trying to achieve. Women (and others) under stereotype threat may also try to control the anxious emotions that accompany their negative thoughts, which unfortunately, can further deplete working memory resources. (Fine 2010, 33; parenthetical original)

What's more, when we take into account the lack of confidence that stereotype threat also creates, from a purely neurological and psychological state, it's likely that those studying, working under pressure, or those facing scrutiny will be in extra-heightened states. For women who have established themselves to a level of superior confidence in their careers, the effects of stereotype threat may die away. In our interview, Sylvia Massy commented that she thought that she might be past this, and Hillary Johnson supposed that it might be more difficult for women first starting out. Fine explains how this interplay with stereotype threat and confidence works:

It's important to bear in mind that these jittery, self-defeating mechanisms are not characteristic of the *female* mind—they're characteristic of the mind *under threat*. Similar effects have been seen in other social groups put under stereotype threat (including White men). . . .

In addition to clogging up working memory, stereotype threat can also handicap the mind with a failure-prevention mindset. The mind turns from a focus on seeking success (being bold and creative) to focus on avoiding failure, which involves being cautious, careful, and conservative (referred to as *promotion focus* and *prevention focus*, respectively). (Fine 2010, 34; emphasis and parentheticals original)

Sadly, research indicates that those most impacted by stereotype threat are those who most identify or care about the work they are doing. Stereotype threat can even go so far as to cause brilliant people to drop out of professions they love, which is why, as discussed earlier, representation and visibility matter.

We may not be able to fully address stereotype threat and stereotypes in general within one or two generations, but it may be possible to address tokenism, visibility, representation, education, and the sense of "otherness" many face in their roles at present. Many of the women I spoke with were unfamiliar with the term *stereotype threat*, and for some it may have been the first instance in which they'd ever been asked to reflect on it. For those mentoring, those in hiring, and those in various areas of education, it is my hope as we move forward and construct teams that there can be more awareness of how stereotype threat will impact their teams, colleagues, and mentees. Perhaps then we can collaborate on new strategies to dismantle these scenarios.

Most of the women interviewed here, if not all, started their careers before the Internet developed into what it has become today. Presently it provides so much visibility. I was curious to see how they flourished, and under what circumstances, and how they viewed their experiences. I wanted to know who had mentors and if they had chosen them. Mentees and students often struggle with knowing what to ask of a mentor; they don't know what they don't know. If your mentor doesn't consider you worth mentoring or teaching, asking for help or direction can be complex. I was curious to find out what these women's experiences were like, if they had been mentored at all. Did they find male mentors who thought they were worth teaching? If so, how? This is also important for allies to understand where and how mentorship worked and where it failed. For if we are to continue supporting women in classically underrepresented fields, it is worth taking a look at what they struggled with at the earliest stages of their careers.

It matters how mentors, educators, and peers in audio and music approach how they communicate about the women they work with if they want to foster allyship and aid in making steps toward change. We know through countless other studies that women's and girls' experiences in education, both formal and informal, are often different than men's and boys'. While that is beyond the scope of this work, it is worth reflecting on how we can continue to support the advancement of women and those marginalized, with an understanding that mentorship is a component of their advancement.

Sadly, a lot of the women interviewed herein had little to no mentorship, and as more women progress through this field, a variety of patterns will likely emerge. For now, we can look at the experiences of the women interviewed here and what their reflections are on them. It would also be worth noting that undertaking a traditional university education is a tactic of circumventing a system that classically hasn't seen women as worthy of mentoring or teaching in the traditional studio model. This is perhaps a generational approach, as some of the interviewees, depending on their age group, did note their participation in higher-education programs or certificate programs in order to gain skills and access to equipment.

It is likely that the current generation coming up will turn to things like online education, YouTube, and other nontraditional training opportunities to seek out skills and instruction and circumvent some of the usual structures and the struggles associated with them. If they are unable to afford university education, there is still a whole Internet's worth of tutorials, articles, and even now many software programs even come with some layer of in-built tutorials. Quite a different environment from the one where some of these women started, having none of these resources.

Where there's a will, there's a way, which flies in the face of those who would suppose that we don't see women in the field because perhaps they're not interested. Clearly these women were very interested, interested enough to seek out knowledge, skill sets, mentors, work, and training opportunities, some in a time prior to the opportunities created by the Internet, and undertook certificate and university education where possible. Groups like Women's Audio Mission, 2% Rising, and many others are making spaces for women to learn without fear of stereotype threat, find mentors more readily and safely, and gain industry work experience.

Untangling academia and music production is tricky. There is a pervasive attitude in the audio/music-production world that higher education is meaningless and holds little professional value for prospective engineers and producers in the field. Diplomas, the thinking goes, mean nothing because many of the top-level engineers and producers don't hold these degrees and instead learned from their mentors by putting in countless hours, both through hands-on training and individual, self-led study; meanwhile, not all these formalized training programs in music production are able to fully teach what some industry professionals know needs to be taught. Because the studio paradigm has shifted over the last thirty years, it has become less common and harder to gain access to the traditional pathways of hands-on training but not wholly impossible. For women who are seeking both training and authentication of themselves professionally, gaining access to equipment for hands-on learning can be an entry barrier. It seems that some of the younger cohort have chosen to take on higher education or formalized training to circumvent this barrier (I know I did), only to still be met with scoffs, in some instances. Some of the women I spoke with here did mention feeling like the courses they took didn't teach them what they really needed to learn; others said that having taken them they were still met with scorn.

This isn't to say that the way recording and music production are taught is perfect and can never be improved upon. The concerns of the engineers out there are valid and should be taken up with these institutions. I would, however, suggest that we consider whose diplomas we are deriding and why. What biases are at play here? Is this just another level of gatekeeping? Time will tell. Classes in recording and music production are relatively new in institutions of higher learning. Simply put, it is worth unpacking as an industry, the attitudes and standards around mentorship, scholarship, and who and how the next generation of engineers and producers are taught. If the classic studio model is changing, this means that the internships are changing too. How the next batch of engineers and producers are molded is important for everyone, and for the music being made. With new technology, a very different music business, and a shifting global music economy, it is important to think about what changes can be made to pay it forward and protect the craft of recording and producing while fostering an inclusive environment. If current biases are not unpacked, then we lack a clear understanding of where we are as an industry and how we can move forward.

WHY DIVERSITY? WHY NOW?
What do you think is the best way to express the necessity of fostering diverse environments for women in music production when many can't see, or don't believe, that there is a need?

Abhita Austin: Right now, my natural inclination is that I have nothing to say to them. Like, if you don't get it, you're living in a different world than the rest of us. I think the way to express this is to actually do the work. I feel like, once again, creating channels that women can come through, and I think we all can do that. It can be, like, for me, I am working with this collective on this one producer's showcase that promotes women, and so I am not only just, like, helping women in that case, but we do little mini docs on them, and that's pushed through our social media channels. So, you're not just seeing a woman's name on the bill, or whoever the producer is—we do this for the men too—but you're learning about the women. To me, the visual of seeing a woman hitting an electrical piece of equipment, touching faders, that's major! Even when I see it and I am shooting it and I live it, but I never see myself back. Even seeing it, I'm like, "Wow." It's like, I don't see this often. I'm seeing it more often, but just the visual of it is very important. I think that we just have to create channels for women to come through, as women, because we can't look for men to do it, because they don't understand. They don't stand on the right level needed to want to do this, and I don't expect them to. So what do I say to people who don't get it? I mean, they have some soul searching to do, honestly. I've even come across women who feel like they're not affected by sexism, and I come across women who are all about, "Why can't we unite with the men?" And that's fine, but I scratch my head. It's almost like you're ignoring something that's there. We have to call it for what it is in order for it to be better.

Leslie M. G. Bird: For me this is a work in progress. I haven't done it; I haven't expressed the need. Even if it's a work that I'm doing for the AES [Audio Engineering Society], we don't have it in our mission statement. It does not say why we need to do this, but my gut says this is because we only have one perspective right now. Teams in there, there's more diversity of gender, of race . . . The more ideas you get from more perspectives, the easier it is to come up with solutions to whatever problem we have.

Hillary Johnson: Wow, that's a difficult question. That's the age-old question. I don't know how to answer that. I think that there's having organizations like Women's Audio Mission and even AES, which is basically because they're so big, they have to be; they have [to] sort of accept everyone and show that they accept everyone. So you have either extreme: you've got the grassroots-level kind of organization that's teaching women and empowering them with tools, and then you've got the corporate level, "We have to do this because otherwise we will look like schmucks." I think having a combination of those types of organizations represented at different—in magazines or an event or as sponsors for things, I think that sort of thing can prove that there has to be a change. In other words that there has to be an acceptance of women in our industry. It's kind of like the corporate group is accepting the grassroots group fighting . . . Does that make sense?

I think that both the big daddies have to support the little daddies. If these bigger companies, whether they be manufacturers, that are forced, that are asked to not use women in their ads, and they don't because they feel a pressure, so, when they get the pressure and they don't put the women in the ad, and then you also have [an] organization like Women's Audio Mission supporting them, right? That sort thing is showing the rest of the industry that there's a problem and we are addressing it and we are making it better, and I think the idea of showing that we are trying to make it better will make it better in the end. Rather than saying that there's no problem, I think that the people that don't know that there's a problem, they're not going to see it. They are never going to see it or it's going to take a really long time for them to see it, and I don't think that they're the ones who should be targeted. I think they're going to just have to be the ones to eventually say, "Oh, yeah, Led Zeppelin—they're not so bad . . ." Eventually these people will come around, or they'll be dead. I think people's individual pressure to not get left behind is pretty powerful.

Sylvia Massy: Any time I have an opportunity to talk to a woman about the job, I'll tell them this one thing: they need to be self-sufficient, basically. So, as they learn how to use equipment, hopefully they will be able to buy their own equipment, not depending on anyone else to supply the equipment that they need. That way if they have, let's say, a laptop, an interface, and microphones, they can go and record anyone. Maybe that's when you're starting out, and I could show them how to do certain things, or anyone could show them how to do certain things, but it's really about experience. So I suggest that anyone, woman or man, get the equipment that they would need to do recording and solicit every band that they could possibly get, every musician to record. So you build up your discography right away, build up your own personal experience right away. I also suggest that any man or any woman getting into the business be prepared to be able to play music somehow, whether it's singing, playing drums, playing guitar, piano. I suggest that's [an] extremely important thing; so [if] that they can improve themselves at all, it has to be that they play an instrument. The other thing is . . . to not be offended and to learn how to take everything that they might believe as an insult with a grain of salt. Let that stuff roll right off your back. You'll just have a better life that way, because you know people get very upset and angry on perceived insults that actually, probably, if they just ignored [them] would not become an issue. So learning to basically not be offended and accept the fact that men are men and women are women, so we're different; we're not the same. We have different equipment, and perhaps, one other thing that would help is to not dress—you know, I used to do this, too; it's changed now. But I used to dress in a kind of a down dressing. So it's not to be too showy, because you want your musician to be the star. You're gonna dress down; you're not gonna show off. For years I wore a T-shirt and jeans to the studio. Now I dress up and wear heels, and I will wear a skirt whenever I can, but it may not be appropriate. I kind of gauge the appropriateness of how you dress in the studio. It's an issue that women have more than men, because men generally have to wear that kind of uniform, and women have more choices of what to wear; so make some wise choices there. As far as me taking on mentoring someone, I'd be glad to mentor where I'm at, but I can't actually support a person by paying them or anything, so I generally tell anyone who is interested in learning that they need to move to where I live, set up, and find a way to support themselves and then come on over and you can hang out, you know? We'd be glad to have a friend; there's no guarantees that there's going to be any work. There's no guarantees that you're going to get anything out of it. But you just have to take that risk, on your own.

Johnette Napolitano: Nope.

Kerry Pompeo: That's a good question, because when I graduated SAE, many moons ago, I went right to work. I was actually the only girl that graduated. I had a very small class, and there were a couple other girls that started the program and for whatever reasons couldn't finish it. My school noticed and was like, "Oh, Kerry's doing good." So they always asked me to come back and talk on panels, and they really—like, I was like a poster child for, like, girls. They wanted kids who were, like, coming to an open house to—if there was, like, a girl in the audience, they wanted to have somebody there to represent them, and I thought that that was very important. So I always, anytime they asked me to do something like [that], I always did that. Again, after doing it for, like, maybe like seven years, I think I started getting a little, like, beaten down. It was probably at the point where I was beaten down about the industry—not being a woman in the industry, just beaten down in the industry, just when I was going into postproduction. Thankfully now I am back in music, but I think it was around that time that they stopped asking me to do stuff because I was giving people too much of a dose of reality? [Both laugh] It was like, "Okay, she got enough chick enrollment up!" But I was really, like, kind of happy to be part of that, because I think it's important for people to have role models. I'm not saying I'm a role model, but, like I said before, being able to see a female's name in the liner notes or being able to go on an audio panel where people are talking about careers and there's somebody like you? So that's why I always thought that was important and I do things like going to The Girls' Club and showing them, because they could have gone to another studio where there's a guy sitting in the space to record in. I thought that it was very important that, you know, they come to me, because then they see me pushing buttons and being technical.

It's as important as it is important for life and just for progression. If people don't see and can't imagine themselves in that situation, they're just not going to try. I think a lot of little girls when they saw Hillary [Clinton] running for president, "Now that's fascinating, I never thought, it never occurred to me." I didn't think, like, "Oh, I can't be president." But it just never occurred to me that could be a career choice. You were not able to imagine yourself in there. We are visual beings, so we have to feel like, unless you're like certain people [who] are just real trailblazers, but as whole society, in order to push things forward, you have to see somebody to know. We don't want to just walk into a dark room. No one wants to do that. Probably about 5 percent of people, on a chart in front of the thing, that would actually walk into that dark room. But if they see that the room is—or maybe they hear voices of women on the other side, they want to walk into that dark room. So it's important. People, like I said, it's easier for them to take chances or just to feel like they can do it and be part of it. It's the same reason why we can't have segregated schools; it's just not fucking cool!

Andrea Yankovsky: The easy answer is education, but it's so much more complicated than that. I think a lot of it is women themselves, of getting women in the industry especially. It's not just music production, women in the technical fields like R&D, software, hardware design . . .

that's, I mean, talk about a dearth of women. It's getting addressed now as a result of efforts in math, science, tech industry.

I think with anything, the pendulum swings, and it is a bit of a cop-out to say, "Oh yeah, you're always gonna get your naysayers." How do we speak to them? . . . That's tough. I don't even—see . . . God, that's hard, because I don't actually think it's a rational position, meaning that I don't know that rational argumentation is going to sway them. I'm not saying that we should give up. I am not saying that we should[n't] have rational arguments for that. I think we are starting to get in the area of politics and religion . . .

All those issues [in] education, because that's—I think it also depends on what country you are in. I think it depends on even what genre of music. Because when you're a man—and, I mean, not to make gross generalizations about who's doing what, and in what genre—but, for example, I would say that people who are maybe trained in classical music have a much more formal education, much more than some people in some more popular realms. Things like that or just from the society that they are coming from. God, it's so complex.

Anonymous: If people don't see the lack of women behind the scenes in music, film, and media as an issue, it's because they don't want to see it or they have a vested or monetary interest in not seeing it. Women hear differently than men. That alone is enough of an argument to turn the 5 percent of female producers into 50 percent, because there's potentially so many different sounds and ideas we're missing out on. There's nothing about men that makes them inherently more qualified to work as producers and engineers; they just want to maintain control of the messages being put out. By including women in the media-making process, we can break down barriers of understanding between men and women, change culture and the way women are perceived.

MENTORSHIP AND ROLE MODELS: MALE ALLIES, CHOOSING MENTORS, AND THE LASTING IMPACT ON CAREERS

How do you think mentorship and role models will help current and future women in music production? What would or did you benefit from when starting out?

Abhita Austin: I think it's major. Once again, that visibility is very important, and even if you don't personally know the woman, just being able to see . . . a woman do something that you want to do, that's game-changing. I don't think I had that coming up. I think it's very important. It inspires you. To me, I get the most of my inspiration from other women who are doing great things, for whatever reason, I guess. For some women, it's not like that. But for me, I am always in awe of other women who are doing great things, so I think it's important. And then if you actually know the person or mentor a younger producer or [are] mentored by another woman producer, that's even more . . .

> **Kallie Marie:** They've done a lot of research on the cognitive impact, especially on very young developing minds, to have that patterning, because if you don't see it, you don't know who to pattern or who to be. So I am always amazed that any of us who were in it that had no one to see doing it, did it. Like, where did that come from? We must be aliens! Where did we get that? Following on from that, what would you have benefitted from, or what did you benefit from, when you were first starting out? What did help you?

Abhita Austin: What helped? They weren't men but other mentors, for sure. School was cool. I went to NYU Steinhardt. To me it was fine. To me, honestly, it was not worth the money. I'm still paying for it. To be honest, it was because they didn't have the equipment, really, to match what they were teaching. They didn't have the equipment that would get us up to speed so that when we left—say, like, if you went to Full Sail, you were on an SSL [brand of recording console], you were on a

Neve [brand console]. We didn't learn any of that equipment. So when I went into the studio, I learned that. I didn't even know what an SSL was. I didn't know all these names. I learned the majority of what's important as an engineer and even beyond the technical, how to deal with clients, how to carry yourself in the studio, how to run a studio, because you are doing everything by the time you became an assistant, you knew how to run the studio. So I feel like interning at a professional recording studio is so important. So I did benefit from being mentored, loosely, by other techs and other engineers working at the studio that I started at. They were men; they were all men.

> **Kallie Marie:** What kind of things did they do that were particularly helpful for you as a woman? Anything that you felt was unique or just in general?

Abhita Austin: They were helpful, still helpful. Nothing unique. They would show me the equipment, how the room works, show me . . . You know, they were open to teaching me. There was no issue with, in particular, with me being a woman. They were open to it. I feel like more of the pushback came from management, who I had tell me that I wasn't an engineer. Which is crazy. Nuts. Like, "Who—why would you even?" Nuts. What would I have benefitted from? It would have been great if there was another woman who was the bomb; but, like I told you, there was another woman there, but she wasn't really focused in on that, which is fine. She was doing her own thing, trying to survive, herself. Flourish. It would have been great, but, you know, shoulda-woulda-coulda, right?

I think what would have helped was if the program that I was studying under was better. That would have been huge. I didn't think that the professors [were] good. There was one great professor, but the equipment was not up to speed. And I paid for it! And I am still paying for it!

Leslie M. G. Bird: It's sort of the Wonder Woman phenomenon: if you see a female superhero, will you put on a cape too and fight crime? Or do you really need . . . that superhero villain to be a woman? A female Superman! It's not fair to say that all women think the same way. It's not fair to say—I don't think it's fair to say either statement. So if we say more women serve as role models for all girls who want to get into meter correction, that's very different than saying it's helpful to girls who need female role models. For me personally, coming up, it wasn't a woman in audio who I looked up to who got me interested in audio; it was the fact that I wanted to do it. I think we have to consider the viewpoint of the person who reads that inspiration.

> **Kallie Marie:** What would you have benefited from when you were starting out, or what things can you think of that helped you in your career?"

Leslie M. G. Bird: I sort of always wondered how a couple of friends of mine got this awesome internship. How can I have gotten this awesome internship? How can I even, with the different opportunity, and if there had been something like WAM [Women's Audio Mission] or Sound Girls around when I was eighteen, I would have jumped on it, because it's great networking. So I'm glad that's there now. What would have helped me? I didn't know how to get a cool internship.

> **Kallie Marie:** Right. So, that being said, a lot of people would say that, despite all that, you've gotten quite far and you're doing great things. So what things *did* help you? What were the things that did get you to where you are? It's important for us to know the things that are working. There's a lot of us that have been in the industry, like you said, before some of these things existed, and yet we've managed. So, what helped? Something must have.

Leslie M. G. Bird: I think the thing that helps is being interested in what you're doing, and I don't mean that to be, like, politically neutral, because after talking to me, and I've been posting about . . . that I'm not being in neutral here. You really do have to have a passion for it, and that helps. In the 1970s and everything else, people have always said, "You can do whatever you want to; just put your mind to it." Whatever. I don't think that any woman doesn't believe that, because it's instilled in our culture, you can do whatever you want. So, you know, that's what I did. I think that's what helped. You know, those positive-reinforcing messages helped. The thing that I want to be careful of is I don't want a woman who's reading this to think that, "Well, I'm not succeeding, and therefore I must not be passionate." I think we have to be, in talking to you, I have to be careful to say, no, that's not my point at all. My point is, yeah, there are some roadblocks that are out there, that are real, that are not imagined, but if you don't really want to do late-night sessions and have a stomach for humility, you have to be humble, because you are the vessel which this art is coming through. You have to be emotionally strong, and artistic differences enter the picture, too. I want to say something like that having a female role model would have been the thing that I needed the most, but I'm not sure that I feel that in my heart.

> **Kallie Marie:** Can you think of anything or anyone that was supportive in your formative years that you knew when you were first getting into production? What sorts of people or situations were really encouraging to you?

Leslie M. G. Bird: I think mentorship is important.

> **Kallie Marie:** So, did you have a mentor?

Leslie M. G. Bird: Yeah, I had the team of people that I worked with, a small team, versus a large-team dynamics . . . I'm thinking—

> **Kallie Marie:** That's really key, isn't it? Being comfortable is important for sure. So many of us have had positive experiences at

various stages through the support of men. Was it blind luck, or was it a case of being self-aware of who was going to be open to working with you and teaching you? Did you choose your mentor, or were you lucky to have fallen into a situation?

Leslie M. G. Bird: I think I was lucky. The Education Center in the '80s, and they helped, and probably I would not be happening, and they helped open the door for me.

Kallie Marie: What is the best way, in your opinion, to achieve more balance?

Leslie M. G. Bird: I don't have an answer on that. That's something that I'm researching. I don't even have my own perspective on that. If I have an idea, I would have, probably, but I don't know. It's a hard one.

Hillary Johnson: I think the more women there are teaching, the more women there will be learning. I think that the women that are teaching find a way to also teach their students, whether they be teachers or mentors, either way, to pick their battles and to just do what they want to do because it's what they want to do rather than not do it because they are told they are not supposed to do it. Like, if you want to do it, then just do it. I think that sort of mentality will help put more women in this industry or will allow more women in this industry.

You know, maybe there's not enough women in this industry because maybe not enough women want to do it?? Maybe it's not all discouragement from men. I think that there are plenty of women interested in stuff, but then they get bored because they would rather do something else that they are interested in. It can be kind of boring unless you are really into music. Being a musician is different. But I am talking about, like, producing and engineering; it's pretty specific. Just like any guy or anybody who thinks they wanna be [a] producer, just because they wanna know how to program fat beats, and they learn that there's all this stuff that goes into [it] and they are like, "Uuuuugh, I don't care, forget it, I will do something else," you know? I think that's maybe just true with women too. I dunno know . . .

> **Kallie Marie:** It could be a numbers game. If there's less women at the starting gate, by the end of the race a lot of people drop out, and if there's less at the starting gate, there's going to be less at the finish line, because a lot of people just kind of drop out of the race, because it's a hard race to stay in and so . . .

Hillary Johnson: I think it's a percentage. If you start with nine men and one woman . . . well, if you start with two women and eight men, and you end up with four men and 1 woman, then it looks like you have even less women. In 1993 when I took a course in recording— after I graduated college I took a course in recording—and there was one other woman, and class was probably twenty-five people. Out of all those twenty-five people, I am the only one I know that actually makes records. But maybe I don't remember their names or whatever. Maybe they work on independent records, so I don't know! There was one other woman back then, but there's only four now in a class—like, a starting class. I think maybe it's just interest?

There's also a lot more jobs now. I mean, I hear about people telling me they've got some live sound engineer that's a woman. They're like, "Oh, you must know so-and-so!" No, I don't know everybody just because I am a woman. But there's actually a lot of live sound engineers that are women. I guess that could be because, you know, they can somehow—they are comfortable because it's part-time? Maybe they are comfortable because it's night? Maybe they do other stuff during the day? I don't know. There are plenty of women that are, like, mixing jingles, you know, so I think there's more opportunities, but maybe we just don't see them. You know, maybe there's just not a community on a big enough scale that connects everyone. Maybe we're doing what the liberal party is doing—we are all isolating in smaller groups.

> **Kallie Marie:** That's possible. Speaking of getting your start and taking classes, what did you benefit from when you were first starting out? What helped you in that regard? Did you have someone that mentored you? Did you have a role model in the industry that you looked up to—male or female? Was there somebody or something that sparked the interest for you or someone that helped you along the way? What kinds of things helped you in general?

Hillary Johnson: When I first started learning how to engineer, I worked—there were two house engineers that were both men, that were both very different from each other. One was very commercial-music driven, and the other was very music, like, the-art-of-music driven, whether it was pop or underground or anything like that. And so I sort of learned from these two guys, who were both named Dave; it made things complicated. You know, like, this is sort of one way of approaching this industry or this, you know, career path, and this is another way. So, I think I sort of learned from both of them a way to sort of, you know, merge the two ideas, I guess. And I think that maybe because of that, that helped me to continue on.

> **Kallie Marie:** With this in mind, was it blind luck that you ended up working with them, or was it a case of being self-aware of who was going to be open to mentoring you? Did you choose your mentors, or did they choose you?

Hillary Johnson: Well, I didn't really have a mentor. It's just that I was working for them. So it's not that they wouldn't take me aside, and, like, work on a mix with me. I think the most extreme anything would get would be, "Hey, can you listen to this mix and tell me what you think?" and maybe spend two minutes after listening to it. But I never really had a mentor, except for maybe when I was starting to get into the world of tech and repair. Then I had a guy that I worked for. Again, I worked for him; he wasn't my mentor. He was just my boss, and he taught me a lot in terms of soldering wiring—that sort of thing.

Kallie Marie: But they still hired you, so there's that, right?

Hillary Johnson: Yeah, I haven't had any issues with that, with being a woman and being hired in this field. Again, maybe I am a bad example. I dunno.

Kallie Marie: No!

Hillary Johnson: I don't think of it as luck. I just think of it as—again, it's my personality type, because, if I know something, I am confident about it, and I don't think any other way. I don't think, "Oh, am I confident about this?" I just—I dunno, it just happens. Or someone will ask me a question, and I will have twenty answers. So, if I don't know something, I tell them, "Oh, I don't know about that, but I would like to learn."

> **Kallie Marie:** No, you're not a bad example! It's important in these conversations to have women who are successful in the field and look at why and how so that can inform what other women are doing. They can have the role models that maybe you or I or other women that I have talked to didn't have when we were starting out, because there's always a path, and somebody's got to shine the light on it. So it's interesting to look at the people that have paved the way and got there without a mentor or whatever, and it's important.

Hillary Johnson: I keep thinking of this thought, of a rock star, in the sense that a lot of men that want to get into recording and producing, they want to be a rock star; they want to be the famous one. So they will push their ideas on the artist, or maybe they will try to play a guitar part on the record. The percentage of men that are like that within, just, men is probably 50 percent. Whereas I think with women, generally, if we want to get into this, it's not to be a rock star. It's because we are passionate about it. And I am sitting here thinking while we are talking that maybe that's part of the problem, is that we don't have the aggressive, competitive, whatever [it] would be, pick some fancy word for me to, you know, to sort of propel ourselves, and maybe that's why we—it's not that we fail, but maybe that's why we are . . . discouraged? Because we see all these other men competing, competing, competing, and you're like, "Well, it sucks to compete with you! You're playing, really. I don't want to play this game; I just want to make records!" I've definitely gotten caught up in that. I'll play that game for a short period of time, and then I am like, "Alright, we are done playing games now. Can we just go in our own corners and do our own stuff now?"

Sylvia Massy: You know, when I started out, there were more women in music production. So I saw women. I used to watch women go in and out of the studio before I had ever even been in a studio. I would watch my heroes, basically, walking in and out of the studio. And I would think, "Well they're doing that; I can do that too." One thing that I could do more is just be more visible, and I try to do that with recording videos of me in the studio or going to lectures, going to universities and talking to students or doing workshops where I can meet the women one-on-one and we can talk. Those are some of the things that I do now to try to help the people starting out. Was that the question?

> **Kallie Marie:** Not quite, but that's okay! So, do you think those kinds of things would have helped you if you would have had those opportunities? What sort of things helped you?

Sylvia Massy: Oh yeah, well, it was the openness of just seeing women in that role was a huge thing for me. That was very important.

Kallie Marie: If we have more women in the studio, on the engineering and producing side, do you feel that is going to be a helpful agent of change in the wider sense of what kind of music gets made or the music industry in general?

Sylvia Massy: Right, right, in the studio. . . . Well, I hate to say no, but I think I would hope the answer would be no, because the obvious thing would be, well, if more women are recording, there will be more women's music, but I don't think that's the case. Hopefully there will just be better music!

Kallie Marie: Sure, no—it could be anything, like, any help for diversity, marginalized groups, different styles. It doesn't have to just be women. Do you think it's a helpful agent of change as far as creating more diversity in different types of things?

Sylvia Massy: Well, yeah, just for opportunity for future generations, yes. I think that there is an interesting revolution that's happened now. The fact that you can afford to buy this equipment, whereas it used to be that it would be a secret, a very exclusive club before, and only certain people work on this equipment, because it was so expensive. Now pretty much, if you can put together a budget and buy yourself $86,000 worth of equipment, you could have a career doing recording. I think that there's opportunity for young women to get into this and to create art. So the revolution that's happened now is there's better music, more creative music that's available. Of course, there's also more crap. But if you dig through, you can find this great music. So there's great opportunity, all the way across the board for better music, and women can be a part of that.

Johnette Napolitano: Always the artists. I just liked recording, started out bouncing harmonies on cassettes in the bathroom. I was a waitress; I didn't care about politics. My head was way above that. I kind of can't believe the question?? I just wanted the goddamn best musicians I could find. Period.

Kerry Pompeo: I am still looking for a mentor. [Laughs] Everything I learned was pretty much from a book, from a manual, from a YouTube video, from me doing it again and again and again and I felt like I got it right. I still don't feel like I've got a lot of things right, but that's why we are growing. That's why I want to be a mentor to young women who are interested in it, because I didn't have that! I think part of that has to do with that there's no more, like, big studios, and a lot of us are, like, doing this on our own? Male and female. There are no big studios, like, how you're talking about the hierarchy, the tape op [second engineer] and this and that. There's no more twenty-man teams to make a record. It's usually a producer in their home studio or in a room that they rent out in a facility. So the mentorship, it's hard to come by, which is why I think it's even more important that I'm a woman and that I am all for that, because I do have experience behind me. If I can give somebody a shortcut, behind me, where I didn't have the shortcuts, if I can give somebody a leg up? I wish I discovered recording when I was these girls' ages. They are doing things that I just did five years ago! They're like a quarter of my age! I think it is fucking awesome, and, like I said earlier, it's going to be very different, and it's very exciting to see where the next ten years are going to be as far as that graph, because that 5 percent is just going up and up and up. The technology, people are just growing up with it. Kids are just growing up with it, and there's all those other girls who code. It's—I think it's important too for girls to see that if . . . I don't desexualize myself because I'm in a male-dominated field. I'm not going in with my boobs out in a low-cut shirt, but I got a dress on, I got heels on, and my nails are painted. Like, this is how I go to work every day. Maybe not heels, but . . .

Kallie Marie: But you don't feel like you have to change you to fit anything? . . .

Kerry Pompeo: Yeah! I think it's important for girls to see that as well. Because when I was coming up, that's how I felt I had to be, and I felt that I had to always wear jeans and always wear a T-shirt and always have my hair in a ponytail and, you know, have a crew neck up to here [gestures up to chin] so that there wouldn't be a glance of boob and I wouldn't distract anybody. I was changing me for the situation. Now I am like, "Fuck that!" But again, now I think that it has taken me time to get to that . . . So I think it's important for girls to see that you can be whatever you want, and we are multifaceted people. Just because you like Barbie doesn't mean you can't also be constructing Legos or have a nice manicure and be able to solder. [Laughs]

I think that genders—and, again, we are saying this in New York, so I am sure it is very different elsewhere—but I think gender, the lines are becoming blurred. Boys, girls, you know . . . I think it is a beautiful thing, and I think that better art is going to come out of it. Because when people can be people, if you are not putting them in a box and let them be, you'd be surprised what happens. Not just music. Everywhere.

I guess I had a really beautiful experience just a couple of weeks ago in Cleveland when I was there for my new job to do training. And, like I said before, I have never really had a mentor. I've sat in, because sometimes as a staff engineer you're an assistant to whomever is booking the room, so I've sat in some sessions with some really great engineers. I have some really great friends who are amazing engineers that I've gone to for advice. But, god, I mean, I would think that the mentor picks you? Because, if they don't want to be in a room with you, why would they want to teach somebody they don't like? I've never worked in such a large studio facility where it's like, "Okay, here's the chief engineer; you're working with them. Done." Well, I had that, like, last week when I was in Cleveland, with a mastering engineer, and, like, I was telling you, that was just such a beautiful experience, because I never really had that before, and that's a lot of—almost two decades.

Kallie Marie: So, how did that occur? Was that a natural, organic kind of thing?

Kerry Pompeo: Well, no, because that's a hierarchy. He's the head mastering engineer, and it's part of my job to finish his production masters. So that was—I guess he didn't really choose me, but, then again, he was one of the people who had a say in me getting hired. And he was adorable. He was like, "I was really rooting for you. You know, out of all the people, and there were some really great people, there was something, like, that was a vibe in you that we just felt." I don't know who I was competing against—not that this is like a competition or whatever—but I don't know who I was stacked up against. But I don't have any, like, Grammys on the wall; I don't even really have that many credits. So for them to, like, take a chance and really, like, believe in me—and, you know, they heard all my music; I gave them a whole catalog from, like, when I started until now; I gave them me through the years—for whatever reason, I was able just to have that affirmation that I really didn't have for working in the business for as long as I have.

Kallie Marie: Okay, so it impacted you in more of an affirmation sort of way?

Kerry Pompeo: Yeah, and that was, like, really it—because he was, like, asking questions and then wanting to hear my answers and then being, like, "Yeah, this is, like, how I would think" and, like, "Wow! That's how I do things! I might make you a mastering engineer someday," you know, that was just, like, all things that were really nice and really assured [me] that I am in the right place that I need to be in right now. That I am on the right path.

Andrea Yankovsky: I think it's huge. I think it's absolutely huge, because I would say that, when I was coming into the industry, I had maybe one or two female role models, and another big deal is that having [one], there were many times when I wanted mentorship from people, but because I was female, it would have been awkward and weird. I mean, because I feel, in more structured, corporate settings, boundaries and job definitions are more clearly defined . . . but with music production, need I say more? . . . It can get tricky. So, there was so much mentorship and so much guidance I would have loved to have had. But there were even times that somebody said no because I was female. And not because—but as it was explained to me, "You know, I would have to spend a lot of one-on-one time with you, or something like that; my spouse wouldn't like it," or "That would just be weird." Okay?

Or—and not just mentorship but also peers, just like, people to hang out with! Community! So, when you're working that hard and say you're working in the studio, you have limited time off. Your hours are weird, especially if you move to a new city, to, say, to move to New York or LA, and you don't know anybody, and you're working all the time, and for me the situation [was that] I was working with mostly guys. I would hang out with my coworkers. But it was still a different dynamic. And then add on the extra layer of mentorship and role models. It introduces another hierarchy, power dynamic, expectations, all that sort of stuff. So simply to have competent women that want to mentor, that are invested and engaged—I think it makes a huge difference.

> **Kallie Marie:** What would you have benefitted from—and/or what *did* you benefit from—when you were starting out? Can you think of people that helped you, male or female, and what kinds of things were helpful, or weren't helpful?

Andrea Yankovsky: It was incredibly just, like, working for Zoe [Thrall, manager at Power Station/Avatar] was a huge difference, and that was not by mistake. [Laughs]

Kallie Marie: Oh, okay! That's actually the next part of the question I have: when you are picking role models or mentors, is this something that was accidental, or were you very conscious and self-aware when you picked—

Andrea Yankovsky: I wasn't self-aware; someone made me aware. So when I was talking to engineers and producers about working and getting a job in studios and stuff like that, somebody—it was Rob Feroni?—who was very, very clear when I said—'cause I met him before I went to audio school even, and I was like, "I wanna go to New York!" and he wrote down on a Post-it Note, "Go get a job at Power Station and work for Zoe Thrall." What ended up being really cool about that is that I was so bent on—at that point still a teenager—doing it myself that I didn't, its actually kind of a fun story. So I didn't tell Zoe or Rob that I was going when I went to apply for the job at Power Station. I didn't tell either one of them that that's what I was doing, that I had been told or anything like that. So one day I followed Rob's advice, Zoe hired me, and then one day after [I had] been . . . I got put on a session where Rob was producing, and so I set up the studio. I was standing there when he walked in the room, and he looks at me and is like—and he gave me this [look], and I'm like, "Yup! Guess what??" He told me to come work for Zoe, so I did. Then it was really funny because at that point Rob went downstairs, because I think we were up in what at that time was studio D; he went downstairs to the second floor where the offices were and said, "Hey, did you know?" And Zoe was like, "You didn't tell me?" So it was funny, and it was [a] good surprise for him. But I was grateful that I worked for her.

In terms of an engineering resource, I was lucky in that one of the hard things wasn't so much gender. Then again, sometimes I did get turned down for mentorship as a result of—but there were so many engineers out there that didn't care if I was male or female who were happy to teach and all that, but I think what one big thing—and it spoke more to the studio business at the time—is, you know, when you are trying to learn your craft as an engineer but you're having to work really, really long hours in the studio and you're fucking exhausted. So having the time to get practice time, to book your own things so that you can do more engineering, is really hard. I think system-wide [this] needs to be addressed. I think the audio schools and audio programs are doing a better job sometimes? It depends on the program. Sometimes I think some of these schools are good at turning out really good assistants, and some are better at turning out really good engineers. But then it depends sometimes. I am not even blaming it on schools or anything like that, but just say a four-year engineering program, where you get a ton of time in the studio, ear training, all that sort of stuff, is going to just give you so much more experience than something that is more of a quick trade school type thing that's designed to get you in the door. Now those schools have also evolved in their curriculum in all that has changed. So I am not up to date on how they've changed and what their curriculum is. My point is that people come in entry-level jobs at different levels. When they are just working their asses off to feed themselves and pay their rent, it's a really big deal, and my commentary on that is not even so much gender based, but also its whole economic problem of the music industry being profitable, studios being profitable, and making sure that people who are coming up in the industry are being paid a living wage. It's tough. That's a whole other thing that is a problem. So I think that definitely affected who I was able to ask for mentorship, how much I got it, how much I even had the energy to.

Kallie Marie: Because you had schooling or not?

Andrea Yankovsky: No, I mean [I] had the schooling. And I think that's another thing, where Zoe was really smart. She didn't—one of her philosophies was she didn't care whether or not you went to engineering school, but you had to be a musician. You had to have played an instrument or sang or something like that. You had to have some basic training in terms of music, not the technical side, the musical side, so that you could—you are going back to caring about directors versus producers, you know. Our sense of sight is so much more developed than our sense of hearing in the context of, say, for example, if you give somebody a digital camera versus microphone, right, you are going to find so many more people that are able [to] become proficient with their digital photography as opposed to, say, a sound recording. Something of nature of what senses are developed in human beings but also what is taught. So in terms . . . So she was already selecting for people who had [a] more developed sense of musical skills and senses. Then you take care of the technical, but just having time to develop your sense, yourself as an engineer, because I remember being in the position of saying, "Okay, I know what I want this to sound like. It's in my head; I know where I am at. But how do I get from point A to point B?" That, honestly, that's not necessarily intellectual knowledge; that's experiential knowledge that you sometimes, you just have to go try it for yourself. You can ask people to point you in the right direction, but you have to go and do it. That's how it works in the saddle. So when you're exhausted as an assistant, and sometimes you have to work extra jobs, to pay your rent or whatever, so that's hard. So if you wanna throw that into—that's maybe a tangent, but is that harder being a woman? I have no idea. But I just know that that sort of thing affected my choices for mentorship and training a lot more.

Kallie Marie: Thinking back, for myself, having been in NYC for over a decade, when I was interning at a big studio, what impacted my development a lot in terms of those choices was the fact that I was worried about staying out late because I was worried about getting home safe, and I was worried about getting into my building safely. So it really impacted my decisions, and I would sometimes get—I would just do it instinctively. I would never even think about it. But then sometimes I would stop and think about it, because I know that my male peers were not going to be affected by that. People would try to tell me that, "You know, you just gotta do it anyway," and I did do that a couple times, and I did get followed home, and I did get followed into my building, and I did have situations arise that were problematic. It was like that, I think, that contributed to the fatigue, because it does impact how long I was able to focus and learn on the job, because I was twice as stressed and twice as scared.

Andrea Yankovsky: Yeah, it was the studio's policy to, after a certain hour, I think it was after midnight, was to pay for a cab to the subway station, and that was fantastic. But I was like, "Okay, but what happens when I get to the subway station? How do I get home from my subway station, which is a ten-minute hike to my house, at three o'clock in the morning?" For my own safety, I could have taken a cab. Well, I couldn't afford to take a cab. That or . . . another big one was—and, again, thank god I was working for Zoe, because this was a lot to handle—when I remember when artists somehow got my home phone number and started harassing me. That sucked.

Kallie Marie: Those are the little things that are not always thought of. And I think that's why it's important for people to hear how these stories have impacted our work. Because I think shedding a light on "How can we get more women in audio?" Well, sure, you can push us all through the schools, and we can apply for all the jobs, and we can get there, but there are still things that we are dealing with that people just might not even register to them. . . .

People need to know because people don't think it happens, first of all. Second of all, the women that do experience it, we think that it must just be us or "It's in my head" or "It's not really an issue." But then when you hear other women repeat the same experiences that you've had, then you're suddenly, "Oh, it's not just me; it's not something I caused."

Andrea Yankovsky: It can be difficult to talk about because it can be traced back.

Kallie Marie: The fact that it impacts our work and people are putting a microscope on the music business and saying, "Where are all the women in the studios?" Well, a dark recording studio, late at night, with no windows, that's soundproof, and you're asking me to stay there 'til four in the morning with questionable characters using questionable substances? You want to know why, and then you don't want to even *pay* me?

Andrea Yankovsky: Yeah, and, again, having talked [to other women], more stories come out of really bad things happening. Real abuse crimes against women. People don't talk about that. It's there, and I think that can prevent some women from coming in, or if they experience it then they get out . . .

Anonymous: I think it's very important, because being a producer is not something that you can just go to school and get a degree and do. It requires experience and a variety of skills including music, technical, and people skills. Also, many women don't consider careers in music production because they only see men in those roles. If girls and women are exposed to female engineers/producers, and if we actively document and expose the contributions of women in music production, both past and present, more girls will grow up dreaming of being producers. The idea hadn't even dawned on me until I was in college, and I had been a music fanatic my whole life.

Also, unfortunately there are a lot of producers who are looking to use their status to get laid or have a reason to get close to a woman. It's sad, but there are predatory situations you always have to look out for. So at least with female mentors, there are much fewer predatory situations.

That said, most of my mentors have been men, and unfortunately sometimes women are competitive or not supportive of other women. So I have stopped focusing so much on gender and generalizations and have learned that it always comes down to the individual.

I was lucky to work with some amazing male engineers who have mentored me, and I also naturally kept in touch with nice guys I felt comfortable with and shied away from guys who I didn't get along with.

Many of my early jobs came from male allies, and I'm extremely grateful to them. I got some great jobs through Terri [Winston, founder and director] at WAM as well. But in terms of volume of jobs, probably most of them came from men who were supportive and believed in my abilities or who wanted some "female energy" in the studio. Until the numbers are fifty-fifty, you often don't have the luxury of choosing the gender of your mentor, and I wouldn't encourage anyone to be too fixated on that.

I did recently meet a guy who was eager to donate his equipment to organizations that teach audio to girls, but only under the condition that he had to supervise them . . . He claimed that "WAM hates men" because they didn't return his emails and told me how hard it is to be a male feminist. So there are real creeps out there, and women have to stay vigilant.

COGNITIVE LOAD AND STEREOTYPE THREAT

Many women carry a negative and extra cognitive load while working under the stress of stereotype threat. How do we talk about this and its impact on women in music production, especially for those just starting out? Seeing women in these roles affects self-assuredness and cognitive progression, especially in the very young. How do we highlight this impact and its relevance? What were experiences that helped you, even if seemingly unrelated?

Abhita Austin: This is maybe what I feel like the root of being nervous is, is not being confident in your skill. So I think that opening up a creative channel that teaches young girls, or women in particular, and focus on them, and teaching them in a safe space. Like, it might be an all-women space. Like WAM or Gender Amplified, like the workshops on microphones or songwriting. That was fun; that was cool. It was like a love fest. Ladies—*Woo!*

Kallie Marie: Because then stereotype threat is removed?

Abhita Austin: It's removed; the women are open and comfortable asking questions, I could tell. It is okay not to be good at something, and I feel like having those spaces, and building up women and girls before they enter other spaces, or the real world, or what's more common. I think if you are producing people that are more confident in the actual skill, a lot of things will fall away.

Leslie M. G. Bird: I had a girl in my class come up to me, Music for Teenagers, and she said, "Leslie, [I feel like I] can't talk shop, and they are talking about microphones I've never heard of, and I just feel really lost." It just so happened that the student was [a] female student outperforming her male colleagues, and I told her, "You shouldn't feel threatened by that, 'cuz you have one of the top grades in the class in this case." So I don't know if that fixes it, but what was interesting was that you described in the end that I'm telling you and that she made it a gender thing, that she said, "The guys all seem to, and I don't feel like I'm keeping up." I think that's the best example I can think of.

Hillary Johnson: All these terms you kids have these days. I get it. You know, it all comes back down to confidence and experience. You can't have either of those things without the other. So . . . wow. This is tricky stuff.

Kallie Marie: This is going to be a tricky chapter, for sure. Maybe it's a nonissue for someone, perhaps, like yourself. You're far along in your career. But women that are just starting out, this is going to be more prevalent for them, especially if they happen to be an ethnic minority as well or maybe they are of a different orientation, a person in the trans community, or a different religion. This is going to impact them in the studio space that is, for the most part, has been mostly male, and in some styles of music mostly White men. So it could impact the people starting out. And I was curious to find out if you had any thoughts on this impact.

Hillary Johnson: It's tricky. I mean, I've definitely done that or felt that, but not, I don't think, with regard to my job, while I am doing it. I don't think I've experienced that. But I have experienced that in other areas, so I understand what it is, and I am thinking . . . how do you get a person to just be completely confident with being themselves when they know that everyone around them is judging them or they think that everyone around them is judging them? I don't know other than bonding or just spending time, like, showing your peers that you either know what you are doing or are confident at whatever the task is. I don't know how you . . . I don't know. [Laughs]

Kallie Marie: I do think that this entry barrier is perhaps one of the last great hurdles, as it were, for a lot of women and minorities starting out in this field.

Hillary Johnson: You know, we are taught to be passive, and we are taught to be agreeable, and we are taught to be all these things, even on a really subconscious level, and I think . . . Geez, I don't know.

Kallie Marie: There's also the technological aspect of it, where, again, like you've been saying, confidence is a huge part of the puzzle, and if we are constantly told that "Women aren't technological," and then you add stereotype threat to that? I am aware of the fact that I am not supposed to be good at technology and I am in a technical environment, where, let's face it, stuff goes wrong in the studio, and that's just part of the job. But then you're, at least from a lot of the women that I've spoken to, some are saying, "Yeah, you know, I'm constantly worried if the gear fails they're going to think it's because I am a woman, and where if that were happening to a man, they would be like, "Oh, this is some really complex stuff; I will give him a minute to figure it out."

Hillary Johnson: No, I think men are just as concerned about that. They are going to think something else. "Oh, maybe they think I am too skinny and I'm not strong enough and I'm not man enough to know how to deal with this." That's crap. Men are just as hung up on what other people think as women are. But I hear what you're asking, and I don't have an answer.

I don't even have an opinion, because that's such a tricky—I feel like that's an individual—every individual is going to have a different quest, you know what I mean? And I think, depending on what kind of support they get, as they were learning, anything they learn, whether it just be, just know, "Here's what a computer is; here's how you use it; to here's how to mic a drum set and have proper phase relationships." Maybe what we need to do is to hire men to work alongside all the teachers that every single woman had in their life. It's a good confidence building thing. [Laughs] I don't know! I mean, I also only dated women for, like, twelve years, so I didn't take discouragement from men the same way that perhaps women who were potentially in an abusive relationship did. You know, if there's women who are in a relationship with a man who's not supportive of her, or with a woman who's not supportive of her, or is single and have friends that don't give a crap about her, she's not going to have any kind of confidence; she's not going to learn her trade, you know? It just won't happen. Then you have all these things that we are talking about happening. So the problem is really not inside of the industry; it's everything that's external. So it's like talking about how to fix the world. [Laughs] I don't know! I think that's a question for the twentysomethings to figure out. How to solve the problems of . . . I don't have any more answers. You're making me sad now.

Johnette Napolitano: I didn't even have time to ponder this sort of thing. I was either writing, working, selling my car, doing whatever it took. You can't just "start out" in music production. Depending on the genre, I would want many years of experience out of a producer.

Kerry Pompeo: That's, like, a heavy weight. I can say I definitely felt that burden, but that just made me work harder. If you know that you are going to be in a situation that's going to be scary, you have to pre-pare for it. That's the only way that things are going to be less scary.

When you are walking into a studio for the first time . . . ask questions. That's what it is. Ask questions. And it doesn't have to start out with a question saying, like, "I don't understand this; what does it do?" Ask—people like to be asked questions. I am actually really enjoying this right now. Like, I've never had such an in-depth interview. So, ask them questions, and if you have to break down the barrier, ask them how they got into the business. Opening the dialogue, you're asking questions, you're getting into the routine of asking things. When it gets to the point that you have no clue about the gear that's in front of you, it's just like another question to roll off. Being not afraid to ask ques-tions is the biggest thing, and if you are afraid to ask questions, write them down and then google it in your phone and go to the bathroom and look up the answer!

There's no excuse to be scared anymore. Ten, fifteen, twenty years ago, I think that there was a little bit more; you had to break down barriers, and you had to ask people or read a book. You can only learn so much from books, and a lot of it is in practice, and you just can't be scared. Especially when we are dealing with technical things. People love to talk. I mean, any situation that I've encountered, we are all nerds; nerds like to talk nerdy things. Get them talking about something they like . . . and then your questions, they might answer your question. Biggest thing is you can't be afraid to ask questions. Ask them to talk about anything, everything, and maybe they will answer your question in the process. That is what I think holds back a lot of girls and women, because they are going to be perceived as not knowledgeable. Well, you are going to be not knowledgeable if you don't ask the fucking question. So, either way, you're doing yourself a detriment.

Anonymous: I'm not sure how to answer the first part, but, yes, I definitely experience stereotype threat and often feel confused whether someone is treating me a certain way because I'm a woman or because he or she is just an asshole. Or I beat myself up if I don't know something and then feel relieved when a male coworker also doesn't know. Or, like previously mentioned, I feel I'm representing all women in that role, so if I fail, it will look like a failure for all women, but if I succeed, I'm merely proving that women are equally capable.

I'm lucky that my parents had three daughters and encouraged us all to embrace science and technology and never let us make excuses for being girls. I grew up with a weird obsession with doing things that guys like to do, breaking into their realms . . . surfing, playing guitar, snowboarding, sound engineering, producing. But I never considered being an audio engineer or producer until I was in college because I had never seen or heard of a woman doing it. And I think most children don't know what a music producer is because it's such a nonspecific title.

WHAT CAN WOMEN CHANGE IN MUSIC, SOCIETY, AND THEMSELVES BY BEING PRODUCERS AND ENGINEERS?

When women are producing and recording other women or any other marginalized group, it can be a useful agent of change, helping to tip the balance of what has been for so long a very White male (from recording studio to record label and back again) opinion of what is commercially viable. What can female music producers change for others by being in this role and, in the wider sense, for music?

Abhita Austin: I think maybe it's our authentic voices. I feel like we're women and we produce, but we are more than women. What do we have to offer? I think that we have to offer the same thing anyone else would have to offer: just our authentic voices. And I guess keeping that voice pure and unaltered by what we think it should be or catering to a certain male gaze. And thinking that it's going to propel us forward instead of just doing the music that we authentically channel.

I think hopefully we could bring more women, hopefully we can bring more visibility to a wide variety of women artists, as producers. I think vice versa, what I am seeing, which in a way is unfortunate, I am seeing more women producers in popular music working with other women artists, and those women artists aren't shouting them out or bringing visibility to them. You would not know unless you looked up credits or you are in line with a certain search on Google or Instagram. But, like, they're not showing any love to the women who are producing their music, and I am surprised! You would think? It's a double-edged sword. Because a lot of women who are prominent, the pop artists that people know, you know that you don't know the women as producers. Usually I find it's like those women have more power in a sense, to bring more visibility to women, who are behind the scenes in a sense, and no one sees their faces.

Johnette Napolitano: Pleeeeeeease. Women are *not* kind to other women in this business. I could write a book on that.

Anonymous: In terms of what's commercially viable, women can produce, but it still won't matter if the record labels with tons of marketing money don't want to pay attention to them. We can't ignore that media conglomerates have destroyed diversity of music, and pretty much two or three large record companies are responsible for essentially telling people what they should like. Until more women infiltrate those positions of power in the business side, not much will change. Producers don't have that much control; it takes a lot of time to both produce and do marketing.

But by putting more and more music out there and declaring themselves as producers, we can chip away at these power structures. By being in this role, female producers can show that it's not just a male job and will offer a different perspective on sound and artistry. Maybe more artists will be chosen based on merit and talent than just sex appeal.

4

ACCESSIBLE TECHNOLOGY

The Great Democratizer?

Historically, recording equipment and associated technology were neither affordable nor small. This has rapidly changed over the last twenty years, and with it, the music and recording industry have been drastically altered. A knock-on effect is the democratization of music production and its accessibility for many. How did these veterans whom I spoke with view these changes and shifts, and what did it look like to them? What did it change, if anything, for them? Some noted that there was less gatekeeping and that there was also better access to some of the tools, equipment, and training resources. While not everyone I spoke with was part of the same generation, and so in turn were affected by these changes differently, there was definitely a sense that the industry changes had mostly been for women, allowing better access to these tools, distribution models, visibility, and the myriad of training opportunities online. Although these engineers and producers may have started their careers at different times, they all share the visibility that the Internet and social media allow today.

Music production is highly technical, requiring a level of comfort with computers, and is a blend of equal parts electronic engineering, acoustics, and physics, while also, of course, requiring a creative balance of the understanding of music and a melding of the technical, the creative, and the artistic. There is also a large portion of the work that is entrepreneurial, as a few interviewees commented. One has to have a taste for negotiation, networking, and, to some degree in this day of social media, self-promotion. Decades of back-and-forth progress and backlash have seen many women traditionally discouraged from these fields, and in some cases purposefully pushed out, hidden, and/or denied entry. A recent renaissance in educational practices is born of a better understanding of early childhood education, toys, and their effect on shaping children's aptitudes through life and a revitalization and egalitarianism in the areas of STEAM and STEM in many educational institutions. In this section of the book the women shared a lot of insights about their early exposure to technology and what kinds of things helped them discover music technology and recording.

In 2105, Dr. Elizabeth Sweet (a sociologist) gave a TEDx Talk about the history of gendered toys and their impact on children. Her lecture shows historically toys have gone through periods of being less gendered and more gendered and that this shift has a very real impact on childhood development and the careers people pursue later in life. How a society educates different people and classes will impact aptitudes in certain areas (Sweet 2015). Furthermore, in *Delusions of Gender: How Our Minds, Society, and Neurosexism Create Difference*, psychologist Cordelia Fine writes that the development of early cognitive stages and social cueing help children learn about themselves and what is communicated to them as being acceptable interests for their gender. That is, if a society codes that certain interests are gendered, then there is a pattern at the onset of what coding young girls have communicated to them about sciences, math, the arts, and technology. While our society's understanding of early childhood development and educational practices are changing, those working today will have received different and varied social coding and conditioning about what fields of interest are appropriate for women, and since the demographics of the people here under interview are from a selection of two to three different generations, we can also see patterns and developments.

Early childhood development, play with certain toys, early exposure to a wide variety of subjects, including STEAM, and positive educational reinforcement all contribute in part to what aptitudes children
will later exhibit. In the last forty to sixty years of public education,
technology's integration into schools and how it is taught has changed,
just how toys and early childhood development are now beginning to
be understood. Some of our understanding of the coding of social cues,
however, has not yet been fully embraced and updated. For example, are
subject areas like math, the sciences, and technology still subtly coded
as being "for boys," either by marketing, overgendered color coding, or
by instructors themselves?

For example, take a look at how holidays like Mother's Day and
Father's Day gift recommendations are stereotypically treated: Mothers
get flowers, scented candles, and jewelry. Fathers get sports-related gifts,
technology gadgets, and alcohol. Its subtle but not-so-subtle gender
coding: *Technology is a man's domain*. I'll never forget while attending
university; I had wanted to purchase a few music production and audio
magazines for research and study. I couldn't find them anywhere in the
bookstore. I finally asked a shop assistant. I was told, "Oh, that's under
'Men's Interests.'" Gendered coding in our societies persists today, at a
subconscious level, and children especially pick up on it in the stages
of development where they learn to categorize the world to help them
order information and develop their own sense of identity.

How, then, did these prominent women in music production experience early education and gain exposure to areas of STEAM? What
shaped their discovery? What common experiences did they share in
these stages, if any? Many of the people interviewed said that an early
exposure to technology and the sciences either made them more comfortable or more familiar with the future tools of their trade, adding that
comfort and familiarity are the building blocks of confidence. Many
commented that confidence was a huge component of success in music
production and the recording studio.

How, then, do we teach confidence? Outside of it being a character trait, confidence in technology and the sciences seems to stem from familiarity and comfort with the subject matter. A willingness to be both curious, creative, and possibly a willingness to take apart and break things seems also to have been a common trait among the interviewees. Ebonie Smith did raise a good point during our conversations, that it's important to let women fail. This is an important reflection when we are talking about educating young girls and women in areas of science and technology. The fear of breaking things often comes up in the discussions. This too is partly determined by how young girls are raised in a given culture and affects their confidence once they are students and perhaps even in the workplace.

Reshma Saujani, founder of Girls Who Code and former US congressional candidate, gave a TED Talk in 2016 called "Teaching Girls Bravery, Not Perfection." Girls, she says, are taught to avoid risk and failure, while boys are allowed to break things, mess things up, experiment, and take risks. Society tends to champion risk-taking men. "At the fifth grade level," she says,

> girls routinely outperform boys in every subject, including math and science. So it's not a question of ability. The difference is in how boys and girls approach a challenge. And it doesn't just end in fifth grade. An HP report found that men will apply for a job if they meet only 60 percent of the qualifications, but women? Women will apply only if they meet 100 percent of the qualifications. *100 percent.* This study is usually invoked as evidence that, well, women need a little more confidence. But I think it's evidence that women have been socialized to aspire to perfection and they're overly cautious. (Saujani 2016)

So with the backdrop of a deeply ingrained socialization of gendered perfection, this socially conditioned chivalrous protection of women from failure—and the good old "I can fix it for you" attitude, at the expense of teaching women, for example, how to wire it them-selves—becomes more of a hindrance than a help. Do we end up with women who are less confident, ill at ease with imperfection, risk-averse, and, in turn, uncomfortable with experimentation, either creatively or technologically? How, then, does the person overcome a lifetime of so-cial conditioning to be cautious and deferential, all while experiencing the psychological juxtaposition of "stereotype threat"—that is, you have to be perfect and be the best because you are representing your entire minority and everyone already expects that you can't do it? *Paralyzing* is a word that comes to mind.

So, what shaped the discovery of music production for these people? It seems that many of them either grew up in an environment where they were either given technological and scientific toys to play with, or were given the tools of trade by their parents, either indirectly or directly, at quite an early age, making these types of subjects and objects both familiar and comfortable. They all shared a love of music and a passion and curiosity for technology and recording. The passion for music, the intense curiosity, and an encouraging environment seemed to be a key factor for all the engineers and producers who were interviewed.

HAS MORE-ACCESSIBLE TECHNOLOGY DEMOCRATIZED MUSIC PRODUCTION FOR WOMEN?

In what way has modern music technology — DAWS, mobile recording, more affordable recording technology, et cetera — and its accessibility democratized music production for women so far?

Abhita Austin: Oh, well, I think it's kind of universal for everybody that music equipment is cheap so you have access to it. I think that's how you find more women who are able to start in production. Like, when I was teaching at NYU, I think when I first started it was 2011, 2012? I remember there weren't as many producers. Just in general,

people weren't really knowing about production. Each year, more people knew about production, and then we would have, like, maybe the
third year, the standout producers were women. And so, in general, I
think it's beyond the differentiation of genders. But what I think is cool
about it is that it, stereotype threat, is removed because you can have
[Apple's] GarageBand [DAW], you can have that in the comfort of your
home, and you can get really good at it and gain confidence in that and
then move that to the next level.

Leslie M. G. Bird: There's no brick and mortar to break into. There's
no gender barrier to downloading Logic and Ableton [DAWs] or plug-
ins. So I think that's good, whereas before maybe you had to worry
about, "Who's going to let me in the door or what?" Now it's easier for
you to have access to these tools.

Hillary Johnson: Oh, I think it's made it a lot easier for women to get
into stuff, because anybody can have a computer, and anybody can learn
how to use a computer. There's YouTube, you can watch videos on how
to do stuff, and you don't have to necessarily talk to other people to learn
something. You should, but you don't have to. You can totally be self-
taught in this realm of music writing and music production these days.

Johnette Napolitano: I have a friend, Horizontal Paul. Bedridden.
Records on his back. ADAT and Roland gave him gear. He can't get out
of bed, but he makes the most beautiful music.

Andrea Yankovsky: It's democratized it to a high degree in terms
of making it accessible. The more we get women designers, women

programmers, that's going to help a lot more too, because when you think about it, basically a lot of the technology was designed for men. I even remember not—I'm short . . . you know reaching the far corners of the console. [Laughs]

> **Kallie Marie:** Me too! Then you are very much leaning over, and that's a whole other . . .

Andrea Yankovsky: Yes, and you start to wear turtlenecks in summer. [Laughs]

> **Kallie Marie:** And you may have a whole room of men sitting behind you . . . and you are . . .

Andrea Yankovsky: Yeah, yeah, exactly. So there's that. There's those parts or even just GUIs being designed for more male aesthetics or the way men process and think. I think those are some interesting issues that are going to come up, more and more. I think we will see some changes as we see more women come up on the R&D side, the design side, on the technical side, because a lot of that stuff is designed by men for men.

Anonymous: Making an album has become more accessible for most people, unless you consider the digital divide. Still about one-fifth of Americans don't have Internet access, and many people underestimate the number of people who are computer illiterate or have smartphones but no computers. Phones are being marketed as doing the same as a computer, but the differences are huge. So, while many people are getting more and quicker access to tools for music production, low-income populations, which disproportionately include women of color, are actually falling farther behind faster.

So, assuming we're talking about middle-class and wealthy women, they have better access now than ever before and can realize their artistic visions on their own or in their control. This is due to cheaper equipment, more software available, and access to education online, through community colleges and through YouTube. But to truly hear all voices, they have to remember or learn how to share the resources and knowledge with low-income women of color so they can also project their ideas, visions, and stories into the world.

WHEN DOES IT START? EARLY CHILDHOOD REFLECTIONS ON TECHNOLOGY

Did you have access to some sort of recording or technological toy in your childhood? And if not, how did you bridge the gap? What do you think you would have benefitted from if you'd had that access, and what were the skill gaps you faced as a result? How early was this [exposure] for you? How do you think that this helped you in terms of developing technical curiosity and later prowess as well as confidence?

Abhita Austin: Yeah, I had tape recorders and VHS tapes, and I would, like, record, which is weird, but I would record onto them. In hindsight I guess that's the beginning, but I would always record my voice, record my friends, and I was young. I was, like, five, six—very young. I wish I had those tapes now! I know my voice is super high, but I would just record me playing, and I would record stuff and listen back, and I would always take things apart. I had no toy or anything, but I was always just, I dunno . . . fascinated in a way with these gadgets, and I guess that I didn't see it at the time and put two and two together. Then, eventually, I got those little Casio keyboards, where you could record a second, so that was fun.

Did they help me with confidence? I don't think that they really helped me, because I was just playing around. Maybe it made me feel more . . . it didn't make me feel anyway that I was the only woman in the program, at school. I was used to being in—I played drums, which was mostly men, so I was used to being in male-dominated spaces, so that whole experience of growing up? It just didn't faze me. Then working in a studio, that was different, because I went from male spaces to a locker room, and I am sure you've experienced that. It's totally different. I was just like, "*Wow!* This is what happens?" I wasn't prepared for that."

Leslie M. G. Bird: Oh yeah, my dad had a reel-to-reel machine, so I knew how to thread tape when I was, you know, four. So that was fun. When I was, like, three or four, 1972 to '73. I certainly wasn't intimidated by threading a tape machine. I certainly knew how to do that. I had to do stuff with my dad. I liked recording mixtapes. Imagine doing this when you're eleven or twelve, in 1982. There's no Pro Tools; it's just "How do you get from this piece of hardware to another piece of hardware?" There were all these cables from RadioShack. Finding out "Now I need the name of the cable and stuff," so by the time I started my audio career, I knew what a lot of stuff was called.

Hillary Johnson: I really liked taking apart my cassette tapes. I mean, no, I had what every kid had, whether it's your parents' stereo and/or your own little boom box or something. I had the basic stuff. It's just that I think I wanted to make everything work really fun, and I took stuff apart a little bit and played with it. I had a little micro-cassette recorder that I would walk around and record stuff with or people talking. I never did anything with it, but I just liked recording everything with it.

I had Atari. My stepfather was a carpenter, but I didn't care about any of that. But he did work in television, but he didn't really share that with me; we weren't very close. My dad was an accountant, so I didn't get anything like that from him. My mom, she wasn't technical, and my stepmother, not very technical. We just had a lot of records, and we just

. . . I always listened to records. I think it's really just music. You know, I did have computers early on. Computers became personal computers. I had a Commodore 64. I typed in—I knew how to type in "10 go to 20, 20 go to 10," or something like that, "30 print," and then you have, like, this same word show up over and over on the screen. And that was the extent of it. Then I would turn it off and just be bored.

And then when Apple computers first came out, we had them in my school and a graphic-arts class, so I would learn how to sort of use the computer in general. And then when I was in college and the Internet happened, I jumped right on that! And then I became a super computer, super user, really early on. But as a kid, a kid-kid, anything tech—watches, you know, TV, the VCR, whatever—I was interested in it.

Kallie Marie: Do you feel that having this kind of exposure when you were younger helped give you a sense of confidence? Do you think that that's helped inform the confidence you had when you wound up getting into the studio?

Hillary Johnson: No, I don't think that made a difference in terms of my confidence, but that made a difference in terms of my comfortableness—you know, being comfortable with the idea of technology. But I don't necessarily think it meant that I was competent. I guess, for example, I took this recording workshop after school, after college. This thing where there was one other woman in the whole class. And I passed this course, and I had this certificate that says, I know how to, I [do] recording engineering. And then I went and got an internship, but it wasn't even an internship. I went and got an interview at a studio, thinking that I was maybe going to get an internship, but, basically, they didn't really need an intern. The guy was just being nice to this kid who wanted to come in and learn stuff. He basically said, "Here, go into this studio and do whatever you want." So I was like, "Um . . . okay?" I don't really know what there is to really do, because there's no band to record. So I looked around, and I found a metronome, and I set the metronome in an iso booth, and I put a mic on the metronome, routed the mic into the mixer, and I just listened to the metronome over the speakers, and I was just like, "Okay, so, I'm obviously stupid, because this is all I know how to do." So, in other words, what you are asking is having this background of having tech in my life, did that give me confidence? The answer is no. It just made me comfortable with doing, because obviously there was nothing else I could do. You know what I mean? Except like record myself or something. So, like, I didn't think, like, my confidence level was low, because I thought that all I could do, that just miking a metronome meant that I didn't know anything. But in reality, it was actually good; it was like, "Oh, that's actually—I did something with what was in front of me."

Kallie Marie: Right, you were creative with it. Well, I guess my thinking was, if someone is comfortable, that's the first step because—

Hillary Johnson: Yeah, sure it is.

Kallie Marie: A lot of, at least, it's changing now, but you know my generation, it was—I still know women my age that are technophobes. They're like, "Oh, I'm not technical . . . Ewwwww computers! Gross, icky." And they're not comfortable with technology. So being comfortable is the first step, and my hypothesis is that, if you are comfortable with technology at a young age and you're exposed to it, it's easier to go down a career path that is technological, versus never having had any technology around, it's going to be a much bigger hurdle.

Hillary Johnson: Of course, yeah. I agree with that. I also think that the women you are talking about that say, "Technology is icky or gross or whatever," I think it's just because they don't care. They care about other stuff. I mean, my boyfriend is a total Luddite. He cares about Star Wars toys, model making. He's a tattoo artist; he cares about that.

He doesn't care about tech. Tech to him is a means to an end. It's not because he wasn't around it; he was around tech his whole life. He just didn't care. So if you don't care about it, you're not going to. It's just gonna—you might think, "Oh, I wanna make records!" but then you realize, "Oh, but I have to use a computer? Ugh."

> **Kallie Marie:** Well, again, this goes into a larger societal thing, because it's often assumed that men like tech, and I am sure, as you've mentioned, there are plenty of men who don't. I've certainly met my share of men who are like, "I don't get it, and I don't know anything about it. Please, Kallie, set up my Wi-Fi router." But the assumption is, you look at "Men's Magazines," or whenever it's "Dads and Grads season," for example, it's all tech stuff or sports stuff, and when Mother's Day comes around, it's flowers and chocolate. I'm not a mother, but I want microphones and guitars, too; I don't want that other stuff. I want the cool toys. So I think it's about changing the perception of who *is* technical, and it is true that some people don't care and that some people do, but it shouldn't have anything to do with what's in your pants.

Hillary Johnson: Yeah, that's true. I'm very technical, but I don't like video games.

Sylvia Massy: I was fortunate as a kid to have a father who built tape machines when I was a baby, so he gave me a microphone to play with when I was two, and he recorded me playing with a microphone. So I was very familiar with the equipment very early. Also, when cassette tape recorders were first introduced, I would do these silly little productions with the neighbor kids, and we would pretend like we were in a theatrical show, and we'd each have a role, and then I would put in the sound effects and the music and everything in the background, and that was super fun. So, I did have opportunity to play around with the equipment when I was young, and it was consumer-grade equipment.

But when I was about eighteen or nineteen, I learned how to play an instrument and joined a band, and we went into a professional studio. It was my first experience in a professional studio, and the engineer was kind enough to say, "Here's some faders. You can play with these, and it will do certain things. Like, you could make an echo here; you could make a delay here." And I was fascinated with that. It was something that I wanted to do because I was familiar with the equipment early. So I do think that giving a child some kind of technical equipment to play with when they are young, whether it's a recorder or whatever, it really will inspire them to move in those technical directions. I think that was very important for me. The other side of that is that my mother sang opera when I was a baby. So I had a lot of classical music and technology in my household. Music and the equipment were always in front of me. So it seemed very familiar.

> **Kallie Marie:** Following on from that, do you feel that having that exposure so early made you more confident once you were around the technology later on?

Sylvia Massy: Yeah, but when you get into some of this equipment, you're overwhelmed, because some of it is very complex. And I had to kind of bluff my way into a few jobs, when they would say, "Oh, you know how to use this piece of equipment?" and I would say, "Sure," and I would be lying through my teeth. But I would say "sure" because I knew I could learn it. Given the opportunity, I knew I could learn it. I got busted a few times for that, though; but I always got hired back after I initially got fired. I would convince them that I can learn it. So they would give me a chance."

Johnette Napolitano: I bought right into every innovation there was the minute it came out. I don't do that as much anymore because I know what I'm trying to get and how to get it, and you don't really need all that, not as much as you used to, to do something great.

I will say that, yes, I've had to get my btch [sic] on to some sound men who assume I don't know shit, but it was much more ageist than anything else. I told a crew of mine once, I can tell by what band T-shirt the sound man is wearing how he's gonna mix, so I can deal with him. It very much helps to know technical language and your own sound in order to communicate effectively to a sound person.

Kerry Pompeo: Music was always around. My dad would have the record player and everything—not that that's really a toy, but it was there. I was always into science projects and experiments, and my mom had a whole kit with the microscope and Erector Sets. I had two little brothers, so their toys, I was all up in their toys. I didn't want to play with my Barbies; I wanted to play with the cars and the Legos, the Lincoln Logs, and, yeah, I loved science. I remember Erector Sets, and I remember them because you needed tools in order to build these things. Now kids are building, like, computer programs. I think it's important that girls aren't just given Barbies and things. I cried when my mom bought me a Cabbage Patch. I was three?

Kallie Marie: You were insulted?

Kerry Pompeo: Yeah! I was like, "I do not want this." I didn't even take it out of the box, and she had—you know, it was the year when it was, like, really hard to get Cabbage Patches or something, and I wanted nothing to do with it. My brother Dan got, like, this flaming black horse with flames coming out, like off of its hooves. I don't want a fucking Cabbage Patch. I always wanted things that were, you know, were animal related or things that you could do stuff with and musical instruments. It was just always—it was funny: there was a picture of me, and there was a coat stand, and it's a giraffe, and his tail looked like a microphone. So my hair is braided, and I'm in a shirt that my mom painted for me, like George Michael, all over it, you know, and I am there, singing to my giraffe butt that looked like a microphone! So it's like, music was around, and because I had little brothers, I had access to boys' toys. Maybe it's different if you're an only child and their parents only gave them, like, girls' stuff. But I had a closet that I could dig into when I didn't like the stuff that was put in front of me.

When I went to audio school, using a DAW was all new to me. I was a musician before I went to audio school, but I knew I sucked at being a musician, and I heard about this thing called engineering! I liked certain records where I became aware that it wasn't just all people playing instruments—like, where there was manipulation, in the box, with synthesizers and drum machines and things like that. That's when it became really apparent to me that there's somebody that's harnessing all of this. I had taken a minor, and I was at a music conservatory when I was in business, and I took [a] minor in audio, so I got, like, a little taste of it. But it was completely new to me. I didn't have a—I wasn't making recordings on a 4-track and bouncing them down. Like, some people have been doing engineering stuff since they were kids. It was very new to me, and I didn't experience it until I went to school.

Ebonie Smith: Well, my mother always made sure I had a radio. She always bought one; like, every Christmas I would get a new one. My first one that I remember, it was, like, a yellow one. I always had, like, a Discman or a Walkman. She just kept me with music-making toys. Record players, tape cassette players, all that. And I think that's when—I think that's honestly what planted the seeds, because I was, like, obsessed with the radio, and I would always have, like, a tape or CD. I would always have the boom boxes. The boom boxes she bought in third grade, I still have it. It's a Panasonic. It still sounds great. I took good care of it. But every year she bought me something, music-technology toy or playback device.

It wasn't just record players and tape players—also video game consoles. With me not having a dad, every time something broke I [would] have to fix it, so if my video game console broke or record player broke or my tape player had to be fixed, you know, VCR broke, I would have to fix it, so it helped me really get my hands dirty. But it built my confidence in a way that said that I could fix anything. And I still feel that way. I can fix anything. I could learn anything. I could figure it out, because I had to, because I was in the position with technical toys. You know, you break them, you gotta fix them, or you gotta hook them up, or something gets unhooked, whatever. So, absolutely—I think the more technology you can have around young girls—the Barbie dolls are great, I had plenty of dolls, too, you know. But I think it's important to have a wide mix of talents and skills. I learned how to do hair with my dolls, and I also learned how to hook up VCRs and stuff with my video game console. So you want to have a mix and range of skills, and I think the toys definitely are very important.

Andrea Yankovsky: Yes—yes, I did. Both my parents really loved music. Neither one was a musician per se. We had a full stereo in the house, and we also had a turntable, we had an 8-track. I had a cassette deck. My brother had a cassette deck that he took apart. Actually, my mom has a funny story about how, because I had an older brother, by two and a half years. My mom tells a funny story about how my grandparents had gotten him some cool toy for Christmas and then him telling my mom that he wanted, that same day, earlier in the day, my mom had given my brother a cassette deck, and he was so fascinated by the cassette deck that he didn't play with the grandparent's totally awesome Christmas toy, and they were miffed. So, but fortunately, and I think that's also a really big deal too, touching on that, because I had an older brother that did stuff like that, so I did. And I think, I give it to my parents, of even if I didn't have a brother that didn't do that sort of stuff, and they did, stuff to take apart, stuff to put back together. There was a phone I took apart. And then I would just play with my brother, and I grew up with a lot of boys. So we were doing stuff like that. And then just musical, music exposure, language exposure—both of my parents speak three different languages. So that's just fostering both sides. That's one of the things I continually tell people when they ask why I became an engineer. It really, for me, it really blended the creative and the analytical and the technical sides. It fulfilled a lot of parts of my brain.

I think I was probably [exposed to technology] as a baby, as a kid, being given stuff like that. Right from the get-go. You know, sometimes I would be given the adult version of a cassette recorder, and I had my own, like, Fisher Price tape recorder—the brown plastic one?

Kallie Marie: I had that too!

Andrea Yankovsky: I know we had a record player that was blue and white. The other thing was, growing up in our generation was—we had, I remember my brother got a Tandy? What was it called? The white kind of computer thing that had—

Kallie Marie: Was it like you fed it cards or something?

Andrea Yankovsky: Yeah, and it was—I can't remember whether it was the precursor to Atari? And it's such a nerdy thing now . . . and then we had, growing up, I remember my uncle, who's not much older than I am, came and lived with us, and he brought an Atari video game console. So my brother's really—he's a programmer now. He totally went that way. And so I think being able to follow his lead was good, just having that exposure. I also went to an all-girls high school that was strongly academic, strongly college preparatory, and had at that point, it was such a good thing to get women in math and science, so we had that.

All that sort of early exposure is good, and back then it was different too, for example, the recommendation—well, having small children,

I pay attention to this now, so the current recommendation is, don't give your kids any screen time before two years old. So that in some ways limits their exposure to current technology, in terms of computers and stuff like that. If you're not doing that, so I think people have to now think of technology more broadly or even more or think back to what was considered technology. So being exposed to technology when I was growing up was tactile. It's the same thing to reading analogue as opposed to reading on a kindle or something or your iPad. So I think that those sorts of sensory experiences are huge—the sorts of investigatory experiences of cause and effect, you know, or "Oh god! I took this apart! How do I make it work again?" So I think that sort of is huge for creative thinking for problem solving.

> **Kallie Marie:** I think it makes a difference in confidence too when you approach technology, because you had experiences where you took something apart and maybe failed at putting it back together properly. You get to do that in a really safe way as a child so that when you are faced with doing it as an adult, it's more natural to you. I don't know that all women grow up with that exposure or experience.

Andrea Yankovsky: They don't. And also if you don't have to deal with the concept of how failure is handled, that's a really big deal, too, of whether it's your locus of control of—and being able to use that as "It's okay to fail." It depends on who's babysitting you sometimes. [Laughs] So—and, again, even, I never thought of it that way, when you go back to early influences of who's your mentor, who's your teacher, who do you look up to, who are your role models. You go back to, whether it's your parents or your caregivers as a little kid, of whether they're cognizant of encouraging that sort of [thing].

Anonymous: I played the piano, and when I was about nine years old I got a keyboard with sound banks and some recording and playback/overdub functions. My father is a software engineer, and I grew up in

Silicon Valley, so I was around a lot of computers and cutting-edge technology from an early age. I'm sure the early contact with technology gave me more confidence when starting to work with technology and music later in life. Having to navigate different interfaces was not as scary, and there's a certain intuition once you've played with a few.

WHAT SHAPES DISCOVERY OF MUSIC PRODUCTION?
What shaped your discovery of music production and at what age?

Abhita Austin: It was when I was a freshman in college. My sister's boyfriend was a producer, and I played drums. I was interested in production. I was in the Village, and I was undecided in college in what I wanted to do. I was around all these musicians, and we were collaborating. Spoken-word artists, like all that. So my sister's boyfriend had a production studio in his apartment, so I would sit in on some of his sessions and started asking him to show me stuff. He told me I could take a MIDI class, and I was like, "What's MIDI?" I didn't even know, and so that's kind of where I started. I took MIDI for nonmajors, and I was like, "Oh, this is interesting!" and then I took recording engineering for nonmajors, and I met an old engineer—I forgot his name. He was a really good teacher. He was probably the best teacher that I had, and he wasn't even in the music-technology program. He should have been. He mentioned that he taught at a thing, and he was like, "I'm deaf. I can't hear anything." I mean, he was not, like, really deaf, but you could tell he had hearing loss. But he was really cool, and he mentioned the whole thing of interning, and so I thought, "Hmmm, I need to intern." I had older sisters and they were in TV production, so I knew she got into interning, so that must be the way to go! So I started interning, and it was all, like, it just blew up from there.

Leslie M. G. Bird: I think I was in college. Music composition and electronic music, because I was thinking I could compose electronic music, but I wasn't, but then I saw this program that had music recording,

I'm like, "All that sounds way more interesting." But you know, back at that time, in the '80s . . . the career sheets that you would get had things like veterinarian, astronaut, things like that; they really didn't have things like recording engineer. Enrolling in the major, you know, being an audio technology major, and it was just added. I saw one of those electronic music composition pictures in a course catalogue.

Hillary Johnson: Wow. Well, I was a teenager in the '80s, and '80s music, pop music, or alternative music, either way, was just so different from everything else before it. So that definitely interested me, in knowing why it was different. You know, it fascinated me. Why did the drums, or just why even . . . at the time I didn't really have that kind of ability to sort of isolate something like that, but why does this sound so different than something else that came out five years prior? Why does it just have this fun quality to it? It just sounds so fun! I want to make that happen. I think also I never wanted to play music, but I wanted to be around musicians because I got bored. I would pick up an instrument or sit down at a drum set and play for like thirty seconds and be like, "IIIIII don't like it. This isn't comfortable," or "My hands don't want to go this way," or whatever. But for some reason, pushing record on my little micro-cassette recorder, and then maybe being able to somehow overlap, I had a tape that I think the cassette deck, erase head was not working properly, so I would record songs over the radio from the radio, and I found out one day that the erase head wasn't working, and it had this really interesting combination of two songs. One was just like some dreamy pop song, with a female vocalist, and the other one was like a rock song, and they blended together in this really weird way, and I think that probably also sort of sparked [it] for me. So there you go—there's something for women: we should take the erase heads out of all of their iPods. If I don't sound fifty, I am going to keep trying.

Johnette Napolitano: My dad's family 4-track. Nine, I think.

Kerry Pompeo: I went to school, I graduated high school, I took six months off, and then I went to . . . so I guess I was eighteen or nineteen when I went to the school that I just took the audio minor, where I had the one class in audio. I was like, "Wow, this is just fucking great!" Like, "I need more." So then I went to a technical school. So I was probably like twenty when I was actually getting into the ins and outs, what a DAW is, what are these things with knobs . . .

Ebonie Smith: Probably around fifteen. I went to a music shop, and one of the keyboard technicians was demoing a Roland synthesizer, and he showed me how to work it, and I just got instantly obsessed. It was very expensive—probably three to five grand at the time—and my mother couldn't afford it, but I always knew that I would buy one. So after fifteen I guess I finally got one—maybe eighteen or nineteen— saved up enough money and bought it. It took a couple Christmases, a couple jobs. When I was in college, I finally bought one a couple years later. That was kind of what planted the seed, even though I didn't have access to it. It was the thing that kind of set my path and made sure I got some sort of music-production technology at my disposal, at my twenty-four-hour disposal.

Andrea Yankovsky: Another thing is that I had a coach in a totally different realm. I played a lot of different sports. I was athletic, and so I had a coach that had had a lot of experience in music production. She was a woman. She was actually the person who even introduced me to that side of it because [I was] going to a hard-core college prep school, and I remember [I] was actually interviewed for an article on this, because it was so—god, this is so funny—I totally forgot about this—you were expected to go from college-prep school to straight into college, do not pass go, don't question anything, make the grade, and I didn't do that. That's a whole other thing of bucking the trend. And I think these days it's a little bit easier, in terms of now, more reputable universities have audio-production degrees and things like that. Oh, and I think you touched on this, too—the difference between Europe and here [the United States], of saying audio production and as technical skill versus something that's more holistic. So back then you could go to music conservatory, you could have a music major, or you could have some sort of technical thing, trade school.

So it was somebody that was outside of my school, and it was also hard too because my parents didn't understand what I was doing. It was funny because I got a comment. So after becoming a lawyer, I got the most backhanded compliment from somebody who, whether it was my parents, my parents' friends, it was whoever didn't understand what I was doing and so went to law school and became a lawyer. It was finally something that my parents understood, but the outside world understood, and somebody said, "Oh, I'm glad you finally doing something with that fine intellect of yours." [Laughs] It was really funny. It was like, "Oh, because I am doing something that is socially acceptable, you understand!" Like, okay, so you called me smart, but you basically said that I've been wasting my life up until now. [Laughs] Again, it was one of those moments where you are like, "Thank you?"

Anonymous: Besides the Yamaha keyboard, it was a love of hip-hop in high school and college that made me think more about music production. I started thinking about how the music was made, learning about sampling, DJing, and different recording programs. Having grown up playing and devouring music, being exposed to a lot of computers and technology, and always wanting to stake a claim in stereotypically male circles, I thought, "Why can't I be a music producer, too?"

5

BARRIERS FACED BY WOMEN IN MUSIC PRODUCTION

Obstacles Yet to Be Overcome

Science creates ideas. Science creates ways of understanding. And in the social sciences, the ways of understanding that get created are ways of understanding ourselves. And they have an enormous influence on how we think, what we aspire to, and how we act . . .

This is the role that ideas play in shaping us as human beings, and this is why idea technology may be the most profoundly important technology that science gives us. And there's something special about idea technology that makes it different from the technology of things. With things, if the technology sucks, it just vanishes, right? Bad technology disappears. With ideas, false ideas about human beings will not go away if people believe that they're true. Because, if people believe that they're true, they create ways of living and institutions that are consistent with these very false ideas.

—Barry Schwartz, 2014

Perhaps the most complex of all questions put to the interviewees, the next grouping pertains to subconsciously entrenched societal behaviors at places of work. What remains is to unpack the smaller behaviors, the insidious habits, and the sometimes well-meant but damaging missteps. As psychologist Barry Schwartz explains in his TED Talk and his book

Why We Work (2014 and 2015), humans theorize about human nature and then design the institutions that we will live and work in; so, if a portion of society has formed an oppressive opinion of another group, this oppression will shape how that group works and lives. "It is only human nature to have a human nature that is very much the product of the society in which people live," Schwartz says (2014). In turn, we have some, as he might say, "bad idea technology," determining who is capable of and eligible to do technological work.

So many common attitudes about women's biologically prede-termined aptitudes have been overturned by science, but human be-lief doesn't always progress at the same rate as scientific revelation. Society is a much slower creature. As we learned in chapter 1, misre-membering is in part a psychological trait that is a component of an unintentional bias, and unintentional bias surrounding gender roles feeds into boys' club exclusions and bad idea technology. Recall how psychologist Diane Ruble and gender development expert Carol Lynn Martin have explained the psychology experiment, also discussed in chapter 1, in which five-year-olds were shown pictures of girls saw-ing wood and later mistakenly reported having seen pictures of *boys* sawing wood—their memories distorted by gender stereotypes (Saini 2017, 50–51). It's not surprising, then, that many women who are recording engineers get misremembered as singers as a function of gendered stereotype misremembering. And it is this psychological as-sociation that needs to be replaced.

So, while trying to in-group and relate in a coded environment, in a not-too-dissimilar way to semiotics, which may also include the music genre, women will also be in part battling being misremembered, mak-ing it harder to be thought of when it comes time for hiring or putting together collaborators. It also makes it difficult to accrue social capital if you are not believably credible or, one step beyond, even memorable.

At the early stages of any career, the expectation is to make a name for oneself and establish credibility in the field. However, more challenging still, is the entry into a field by women lacking the types of social capital required to flourish in networking, entrepreneurial, and technical endeavors, often concurrently.

Undoubtedly, music is very social, and this means that, as in many fields, networking is important, if not doubly so. Social capital is also largely at play in a variety of contexts in and out of the studio, like whom an artist chooses to work with, who a label sees worthy as hiring (for those still operating under those business models), and how teams, bands, and collaborations are built. Each of the interviewees navigated these scenarios differently, reflected on their experiences, and shared how this changed for them over the years—for some, not at all. It is important to name entry barriers; for in naming them we learn to recognize them as they arise and build the language to talk about them.

Pay equity was also discussed, and on the whole, almost every interviewee said that the greatest problem with pay in the industry is ensuring that people get paid *at all* for the work they do. This sadly speaks volumes about the plight of music today and means it is unlikely that pay equity can be fully addressed until people are properly getting paid, and on time, regardless of who they are in the industry. In some cases, a variety of factors influenced whether a person gets paid on time. While this is an industry-wide issue, affecting many freelancer and creative roles, there is plenty of evidence that issues at play pertain to pay equity and to women's confidence negotiating salaries. In an article for *BitchMedia*, journalist Sarah Grey writes that currently more women are freelancing than ever before. Perhaps the entrepreneurial aspect of self-employment advantages women who are recording engineers, producers, or audio engineers. Grey writes, "The Bureau of Labor Statistics found in 2013 that, all other things being equal, female freelancers out earned male freelancers by $10 per week. This suggests that women who were undervalued in more traditional workplaces—because of sex, race, parental status, age, gender, sexual orientation, looks, social connections, and hierarchies, or any of the other factors that give men the workplace advantage—earn more when they ditch the boss and take their chances in the freelance sector" (2016).

While the pay gap between men's earnings and women's earnings is now so widely accepted, to the point that we currently have different days of the year dedicated to pay-equity awareness, perhaps there is an economic incentive behind the bold strides these women have made. Even though the industry has a reputation as an unstable Wild West, a place with fast and loose rules, especially when it comes to being paid on time, having a steady income, and the varieties of sources of revenue that people working in the recording industry are paid; uniquely, women might still fair better freelancing, as their counterparts in other fields, than taking their chances in the traditional corporate trajectory. While we didn't discuss the interviewees' earnings directly, we did talk about how they viewed their pay, and it was interesting here in our conversations to see that, overall, a sense of solidarity exists regarding the issue of payment for work. Perhaps that's a strength to take away, this sense of solidarity, a common struggle in the music and recording industry, and a unifying cause.

The discussion also broached the subject of cultural backlash, and I wondered what their own awareness of this might be. Seemingly, progressive movement in society is invariably followed by a period of backlash culture, countermovements, and restrictive reactionary regulations. This cycle is evident throughout much of history. An example comes to mind, chiefly with technology and women, who in the early days of computing were most of the workforce in this field, and it was accordingly seen as "women's work." The Science Museum of London describes it thus:

> Women have made important contributions to computing—manual, mechanical and electronic—from its earliest days. From the 1700s until the early 1900s, "computers" were people—low-paid and often female workers who did the laborious and repetitive calculations

needed for astronomy observations, ballistics calculations and biology. This work was often unacknowledged or uncredited as it was
considered low-skilled. (2020)

It seems that whatever work women do, society views it as unimportant
or unskilled. After the computer revolution, when men began managing the computing, the job status was then elevated, and so, too, followed the pay—a cycle often echoed in other industries where the work
has been predominantly male.

I found myself wondering, "If more women are eventually in music
production and audio engineering, will there be a backlash? If so, what
will it look like?" Without digressing into the economics of different
periods and how they relate to world wars, the workforce, and gender,
I wanted to find out if these engineers had any sense of what may be
ahead. While speculative, I wondered if it was at all too early to think
about the potential backlashes that might come from the present surge
of women's visibility in recording, audio engineering, and music production. For example, feminist author Susan Faludi notes that during
the latter half of the 1980s, "as much as 45 percent of the pay gap [was]
caused by sex segregation in the work force. (By one estimate, for every
10 percent rise in the number of women in an occupation, the annual
wage for women drops by roughly $700)" (Faludi 1991, 365).

Though these statistics are from the late 1980s, the cultural phenomenon continues. Consider the period of US history spanning the
earliest days of mechanical computing in the mid-twentieth century to
the gains women had made in the workplace in the 1970s to the en-
suing backlash of the late 1980s. Some of the engineers and producers
interviewed here were in the early stages of their careers in the 1980s
and so likely either knowingly or unknowingly experienced some of
this cultural impact in their daily working lives, inside and outside the
recording industry. As more women enter the recording industry, will
this pattern repeat? Perhaps it is too early to tell. My hope is that, if we

are aware of what may be ahead in terms of backlash, we may be in a better position to combat it.

Complicating the denigration associated with "women's work," for hundreds of years, beliefs about the "separate spheres" of men and women have been deeply coded and entrenched: men's sphere being work, the world, business, and technology, and women's being the home, childcare, and domesticity. Victorian ideals helped estabish the ideology, which saw a resurgence during the 1980s in reaction to second-wave feminism of the '70s and its attempts at an ERA, as Susan Faludi describes in *Backlash*:

> Beta mode, and other distinctively "feminine" traits didn't occur in a vacuum. In the '80s popular works praising "women's ways" and "women's special nature" began to crowd out other fare in the women's section of American bookstores, works that ranged from Sara Ruddick's *Maternal Thinking* to Sally Helgesen's *The Female Advantage*. The authors wrote, sometimes with starry-eyed terms, of women's inordinate capacity for kindness, service to others, and cooperation. Soon, "feminine caring" became the all-purpose tag to sum up the female psyche. And by the decade's end, some of the authors of this genre (who were largely women) seemed at times to be even actively joining the backlash. Suzanne Gordon, in her 1990 *Prisoners of Men's Dreams: Striking Out for a New Feminine Future*, blamed much of the unkind '80s on "equal opportunity feminists," who encouraged women "to devalue caring work" and "exacerbated a widespread societal crisis in caring." (Faludi 1991, 325)

It's almost as if this scapegoating of feminism's decade of influence has drifted partially into the present, and while more prevalent in the 1980s, women's roles in the separate sphere are still subtlety tacked onto their professional lives today. It's no coincidence, then, that people raised during this time and working today might view some of the value that women can offer in the workplace in the same way as did academics of the 1980s, who "seemed to forget the force of socialization altogether and presented women's and men's roles as biologically predetermined and intractable" (Faludi 1991, 326).

Practically speaking, today "separate sphere" thinking is in evidence whenever it's assumed that a woman's "natural role" is to be a "helpmate" and tend to the domestic needs of the mostly male colleagues around them. This is seen in scenarios where secretaries (predominantly women), for example, found themselves managing things like dry cleaning, the purchase of anniversary gifts for their bosses' wives, and any other personal tasks falling outside the boundaries of their job descriptions. It's still commonplace today for the remembering of birthdays, the bringing of cakes, the washing up of coffee mugs in the break room, and, in general, the performance of otherwise domestic and emotional labor to fall to the women of an office.

So what does this separate-sphere-ism look like in the recording studio? The *studio mom phenomenon*, as I call it, occurs when women working in audio and music production either accidentally or purposely are assumed to fit this mold of domesticity and are responsible for, in some instances, extra emotional labor outside their role. In some cases, these gendered stereotypes result in extra microaggressions to process. For even though seemingly positive, the stereotype of nurturing and helpfulness can be confining.

In some instances, the people I spoke with used stereotypes to their advantage when doing so matched their personality type, and I wanted to find out if they were consciously doing so and when. I also wanted to see how they viewed these scenarios and how these expectations have impacted their work life and successes. Some seemed self-aware about a mentality of needing to be "one of the guys," as was discussed during "Boys Clubs" and "Networking," and have bucked convention as much as possible by making it known that they are tough and in charge and making sure to try to assert a different view of themselves in these environments. It must be very limiting and exhausting to process these roles subconsciously, when the only processing and limiting that should be going on is that which is applied to audio.

Part of the *separate-sphere hangover* I see affecting women's career trajectories, from employment seeking to advancement, is found in what I have termed *glorified secretarial*, where women are othered out of roles in music production and audio engineering because they are helpfully eschewed away to other supporting roles that their male peers see them as being perfect for. This looks like suggesting or directing young, entry-level engineers and producers into management, A&R, marketing, sales, and other desk-type or clerical jobs. Though these roles are vital to the music industry, they are more music *business* and are not technical or creative roles. It seems helpful; it's a job, right? It's music *adjacent*. Getting a foot in the door seems like a good thing. But if there's a mistaken perception that women aren't technical, scientific, or just simply as capable and qualified, then they are steered into roles (however well meaning initially) where they answer phones, write emails, or manage schedules for the team, *not* because they actually express an aptitude or interest in liaising and client-facing work, but because society is a bit more comfortable seeing them in those roles and not as technicians. This in turn continues to enforce gendered stereotypes and ultimately, even though often well meaning, keeps qualified and talented women out of the studio, back behind the wrong kind of desk, doing glorified secretarial work. I am not supposing that people are sidelining women on purpose, especially because the early days of one's career in this field can mean doing quite a lot of menial tasks at a studio, including and not limited to answering phones, cleaning toilets, rolling cables, and organizing tape libraries. Quite the opposite! Rather, it is these deeply subconscious biases at work that we must learn to recognize and unpack so that people can progress past these areas, are mentored, and are thought of for promotions. Otherwise, as Barry Schwartz opines, we compromise the industry with "bad idea technology."

Sometimes women do choose liaising and client-facing pathways of their own accord after years of struggling in the business. More regular hours and more reliable pay may of course be a factor; however, do we see more women drop out of their technical ambitions for glorified secretarial work because it is easier to get these jobs? Just a little less of an uphill struggle after so long of trying to make an inroad, or was the thinking that they could do the deskwork for a time and that it would lead to engineering work later? If people's perception of you is that you are misremembered as a manager or someone from marketing, then how difficult will it be if you are trying to transition into engineering and production, even if you've temporarily done one of these jobs to supplement your income?

How many women have abandoned their ambitions of a technical role in the industry influenced by a widely ingrained acceptance of biological determinism, that women are somehow innately "better at *that* kind of social role and organizational work"? What part of gendered socialization is contributing to the lack of women succeeding in production and engineering roles? If women are not perceived as being technical, then it's harder for them to get hired as such in the first place and in turn makes it more likely that they may eventually accept a recording-industry-adjacent, less technical role.

Perception greatly affects how journalists write about women in these roles and affects their advancement and how seriously they are taken in their careers. For example, questions that an interviewer might ask a woman audio engineer or producer, are not always the sorts of questions that her male peers would be asked. It is time to think deeply about what questions are outdated. How can we move the conversation forward and continue to advance the perception of women in music production and audio engineering to a more equal place? I've asked the engineers and producers here to reflect on what they think should be asked in interviews and what they've experienced to date. *Deprofessionalization,* or otherwise discrediting or making people appear less professional, also falls into this area, and though it was not directly discussed, it is often the outcome of some types of questions or comments made in the media. How are women's professional contributions talked about differently in the media? Not solely a music industry problem, deprofessionalization affects women's contributions and perceptions in medicine, the corporate world, and technology. In order to change society's subconscious biases, we can start by addressing how we speak about people professionally. Colleagues writing referral letters or journalists conducting interviews and writing articles need to be aware of the language used when talking about women's professional contributions and attributes. Saying that "she helped out on the record" when she was actually the producer or the engineer undervalues her professional contribution, demoting her to the role of helpmate. Imagine if men talked about working with each other in this way. What if an artist, when asked what it's like to work with producer Rick Rubin, were to say, "Yeah, he's a really sweet person; he helped out on our record"? While not negative words in any shape or form, it makes it seem like the work was casual, that Rubin's input was incidental and not skilled expertise that should be paid for. It makes it seem that Rubin is a "helper."

Even if well-meaning, language like this improperly skews the portrayal of these engineers' and producers' contributions, undervalues their professional competence, and negatively impacts their ability to get more work. Word of mouth accounts for many jobs won in the industry. Engineers and producers gain clients through artists hearing of their work from other artists or having potential clients hear projects they have worked on, especially when they are credited correctly and adequately, and having their contributions being spoken about in a professional and technical way.

SOCIAL CAPITAL, NETWORKING, AND "BOYS' CLUBS"

Some academics on the subject have posited that producers have the "ability to wield power" in the recording studio and that this is in part "dependent on the accumulation of cultural capital, as well as maintenance of social relations within the field" (Phillip McIntyre, academic and producer, 2008). What are some of the challenges women face in the "accumulation of cultural capital and social relations" that are needed to have this command in the studio? How do you think this differs subtly for women engineers and producers?

Abhita Austin: I guess for me, it might be an initial challenge, or it just might be a comfortability. I think there is a comfortability when you talk about networking that men have with men, and especially in music. For the past couple of years, I've been doing work with the Pushing Buttons Collective and Gender Amplified. I am out in the street a lot, connecting with people, because we are throwing shows, conducting workshops, blah-blah . . . And so I think that, although I am connecting with men and women, but I am connecting with—and maybe I am just projecting—but there is a sense of, in some cases, men not being as comfortable with me or seeing me only in one way. I think it gets back to not being taken seriously. So I think that maybe the challenge might be, even when you are networking and you're connecting and building a genuine connection—because I am all about genuine connection. I can't do anything else! That's a whole 'nother [*sic*] thing. When you are doing that, right . . . you know when the smoke clears, if in the back of their heads men, who I guess might be gatekeepers, they might not be, but if they are, if they're not thinking of you and they are cool with you but they're not thinking of you in that role that you might want to be in or . . . might be beneficial to your movement, they're not even thinking about doing that. It doesn't even—not that the connection doesn't matter, but it's not helping. It's like, you could be friends with someone, genuine connection, cool, but he doesn't think of you as a technical person. So if something opens up, where it's an opportunity and he knows somebody is looking for a technical director or instructor, blah-blah-blah, he would not think of you. That's unfortunate. I think that that happens a lot. I think it's not being taken seriously. Some men, I have to give it to them, I am thinking of one person in particular, they're, like, adamant about putting women in positions, and I am happy and thankful. But there are a lot who do not even see you, who won't consider you. Either they see you—like, I do video as well, so they just see me that way, or they won't consider me for whatever. Which is fine, because, ultimately, I am beyond networking for promotions. I understand that my level of success has to do with me. I have a good support system. But if you are not ready to receive, it's not going to happen. I'm never putting my eggs in anyone's basket.

> **Kallie Marie:** There's definitely some truth to what you said earlier, about being misremembered. They see you as a woman at networking events, and I have had wonderful connections with people, genuine, great connections, and the next time I see them, they ask, "How's the singing going?" And I'm always like, "I don't sing." And they usually respond, "Oh, I'm sorry; I thought that you were a singer. What do you do again?" And I'm like, "Remember? We had that whole great conversation about that piece of gear, and it was a networking event specifically for [what] we do?"
>
> So people constantly, at least in my personal experience, misremember me as a vocalist: "Oh, you do music . . . So, what kind of style do you sing?" Me: "I don't." And then they are really perplexed and silent for a time.

Abhita Austin: I've had people, when I am engineering, ask me, "Oh, you look like a singer!"

Kallie Marie: Yeah, I get that all the time: "You look like a singer."

Abhita Austin: "I am engineering right now. I record singers?"

Kallie Marie: People reach out to me on my website all the time asking me if I will sing on stuff. There are no pictures of me anywhere suggesting that I sing? So I think, at least in my experience, there is a misremembrance. I use that term because people imagine what they think you are based on—

Abhita Austin: What they think in their head—

Kallie Marie: Yes, their notion of what they think women are or do.

Abhita Austin: Stereotypes.

Leslie M. G. Bird: I think you have to not hide your head in the sand and think there aren't guys who are sexist, and so I don't think it's necessarily a barrier, but I think not just being aware of it, there's some guys who really don't think you can do this. Maybe what I am saying is ignorance is bliss. Maybe that's what I am trying to say.

You know, it's real. It's not an imagined thing. Funny things, like the reason that I am doing things like this, that I am still doing this advocacy, is that it boggles my mind that there are still guys who think like that. Red Bull started [an academy] called—I can't remember, and Ableton are looking to have more female-certified trainers. Don't be naive about what the barriers are.

Hillary Johnson: I think they just don't have the same comp—this goes back to the competition thing. I think that what you are talking about is, it's a stereotype on its own. I don't think that, if you are talking about LA, records in LA in the '80s versus making records in LA now? I think that the power factor would be totally different. I think that the power that a woman could have as a producer now would be to non physically spank the musicians—you know, get them to work harder.

I think the actual power wouldn't necessarily come from the attraction to them, like, "Oh, I want to work with this person; they've worked with so and so and so and so . . . and they have cocaine, and they can get me into whatever and buy me beer . . ." Stupid. But now it's more like, "What can they do for me once I am actually working with them?" Whereas I think that the shift is away from the glamor of the idea of a producer. Maybe not in the hip-hop world, but even in the pop world. I think that people are starting to realize, artists are starting to realize, that the producer of their record actually has to have substance. I don't think that these artists are that stupid anymore. They are much more wise, and I think that they know that the producer is not necessarily the person that's going to help them have a career. I think that they know it's more marketing and publicity and all those things, and the producer is going to help them along the way, and the producer may know people. So I think being a man or a woman, I think there's less focus on the glamor of it. Which is helpful for a woman who doesn't necessarily want to compete with those guys who are like, "I know so-and-so. We can go and get into this show for free" or "I will help you book a tour" or whatever.

You know, the bottom line? I think to all your questions is that, and I am hearing myself answer these things, stuff has changed. Maybe not as drastically as we had hoped or as we would like, but I think that actually it has changed, external to our industry, which has affected our industry. So it's just a matter of continuing to do the same things and continuing to push the envelope, chipping away.

Sylvia Massy: You know, I think one of my biggest hurdles as far as networking goes was not being a woman but was because I don't drink. Because I think you could network by going to shows really easily, going to bars, watching bands play, and I just don't do that because I don't drink. It's kinda not fun for me. So that's the reason that some networking things don't work for me. However, there was a good story that I had that I think did have to do with me being a woman.

I was talking with a band called Avatar, a metal band from Sweden, about doing a project with them. They said, "Come see us at this show," so I said, "Okay, I will be there at the show," and the show was in Maryland, Baltimore, and I got there to the show, I watched the show, they were fantastic. I was supposed to meet the band at the end of the show, but they had never met me before, and they were at a table, signing autographs after the show. And so I said, "Hey, I'm supposed to meet the band," and, you know, the bouncers were like, "Yeah, girl, yeah. Get in the back of the line," you know? I was like, "No. I'm a producer. I am supposed to be meeting the band." And they were like, "Yeah, yeah, yeah, get in the back of the line." So I stood there for a few minutes and I thought, "Well what the heck. I'm just going to bust up there and go talk with them." So, I busted through the line and through where all the security was, and I went up to the table, and I said—and I banged my hand on the table—and I said, "I'm Sylvia! I'm supposed to be meeting you here!" And all the security grabbed me and dragged me out of the venue, and the band was like, "No, no, no, no, she's supposed to be here!"

So maybe the guys, the bouncers, think I am one of those girly girls or whatever . . . a fan. I think that my thought then was because I had another experience with a band called Limp Bizkit where I was supposed to meet the band after the show. And I stood in that line with all the girls, and I just got frustrated, and I was like, "I don't want to stand in line and be like one of these girly girls here." You know? 'Cause there's, like, what do you call them? Groupies. There are girls who just wanna see the band, go meet the guys, and I'm not that. So I got frustrated, and I left. I just walked away from the Limp Bizkit project, whereas I could have probably done that record that sold six million copies, but because I was a girl, in my own head, I was offended. That was my problem. It was me that had the problem. There was nothing else that was a problem except for that.

Johnette Napolitano: That's why academics make shitty records.

Kerry Pompeo: No, I think because, women engineers and producers, we are still kind of like Little Gems, that kind of pop up every once and a while. I've always been welcomed in, like, social-networking situations, and I think part of it is just, like, I'm a super nerd and I can speak in their language. I think the real, true audio nerds, it doesn't matter what gender. It's more a matter of, like, do you speak their language? But, you know, there's always, like, because you're a girl, guys want to flirt with you, that kind of thing . . .

> **Kallie Marie:** How is that a barrier for you professionally? We are used to this language, but communicating it to other people, who these challenges would never occur to, and that's the important part of doing these interviews—because we know how it affects us professionally. But until we verbalize it—

Kerry Pompeo: It's like the same thing . . . them seeing us here, they need to hear our experiences, otherwise how do they know what to look out for to deal with it?

Ebonie Smith: I never had a He-Man Woman-Haters Club rejection from anybody, like, "No women allowed." I've never dealt with that. I've dealt with more microaggressions, where it's just, "You're not invited. We are all going to hang out. You're not invited." Which is cool. I think there are [a] couple of ways to deal with that: You can push yourself in—don't be afraid to push yourself in, especially if you know that

that's where the deal is being made and you want to be in on it. Just because you are not invited doesn't mean you can't crash the party. "Okay, I'm here!" I've done that before. Just roll up, "I know I'm not invited, I know you don't want me here, but I am gonna get a beer and try to get what I need from the situation because I don't care if you want to hang out with me." I think more women need to definitely learn to do that.

Also, just crash. Find out where the thing is, and go and get what you need, and try to get in however you can. That's one approach. The other approach is the Gender Amplified approach: Find women who think like you think, who want to be around you. You make friends with them because you actually wanna be there. You don't have to crash every party where there's resources; you can crash half the parties, and the other half you can start yourself and go because there's just as many resources among women in audio as there are among men in audio, if we actually talked to one another. You'd be surprised—you actually have guys trying to crash our parties. Which is the kind of position that you really want to be in. You want them to be like, "Damn. These girls, this community of people that wanna be around each other are awesome, and we want to be part of this!" So I think it's—those have been my two approaches, like, leaning into my community, that I believe in, which is Gender Amplified, women's organizations, and also not being afraid to be, like, "Look, look, I want to be friends, you have resources over here, I want to know about them, so I am going to crash. You don't have to invite me." Nobody is ever going to be like, "You can't be here." It's all, like, discrimination suits. We've advanced enough in America where there are no more colored water fountains; nobody can keep you, legally keep you, out of anything. So don't be afraid to crash the party if you have to.

Andrea Yankovsky: I was thinking about this recently, not in those terms, but in a related way, of how your credits establish your credibility in this industry. People are very concerned with who you've worked with and whether they will respect you or not based on that. I was thinking about that with other industries, where—how do I explain this . . . So, it's an analogy. The people at the top are always going to be at the top. All the industries are going to have somebody at the top, as somebody that has the incredible client list that is out there. The Bob Clearmountains and the Al Schmitts, and all that, just have resumes up to wazoo. So many other industries, you don't have to have the best. Say I'm hiring a website designer. Do I have to [get] the website designer that designed the most . . . won a Webby? *No.* I can and that's—if I am a Web designer, I can also put myself out there and get business and do a perfectly good job and help people accomplish what they need. It could be like a website for a small business. [Laughs] That's totally functional; that's fine. Now, the music industry is different from that. Sometimes and in some ways I think it's good. We do need to have standards. It does frustrate me where, you know, anybody can hang up their shingle and call themselves an engineer when they don't know shit, right? But the flip side of that is that it does allow people who want to get out there and learn and become good at what they do—it gives them an opportunity to go get experience. If you are determined at getting good experience and getting feedback and actually improving, you can get it. So that's tough, because then what happens in the music industry [is that] you're always asked about your credits. That's what gives you power, and getting those credits can be difficult.

You have to start somewhere, and then, yeah, I think it does create . . . a big boundary there. People in the music industry are so conditioned to be like, "Who do you work with?" "How good are you?" "Who do you know?" "Who can vouch for you?" Again, there's good things to that and negative things. This is how it's male-dominated, so I think that can be tough. In terms of wielding power, it goes back to how women are expected to behave or how comfortable they are feeling—the unintentional things. It's so complex.

Anonymous: If you mean cultural capital in terms of the culture a person has, then I think there's not much difference. Women who want to produce can and should learn about and listen to other music and art for references and to be able to be educated when speaking with others about music. But if you mean that in some cultures men are seen as more valuable, then I think the only way around that is to keep infiltrating the industry and force the culture around it to change. Once more women are in, they will start shaping the culture even more based on their experiences, and that may open the way for more women, and it will continue as a feedback loop. In terms of social relations, men are often more in a position of power because of physical strength or stature, but women may have the upper hand in terms of being generally more sociable creatures. Otherwise, it comes down to being an alpha or beta personality type.

IDENTIFYING AND OVERCOMING ENTRY BARRIERS

Women are often not taken seriously, not just in music production, until after they have become established, which creates an entry barrier. How do we combat this type of entry barrier? What other types of entry barriers do you think women face?

Abhita Austin: That's the thing—that's what I come back to. You gotta create it. You know, because a lot of times, that's what I did. I wasn't a barrier, but I was, like, the main engineer at a studio, and then I didn't like the environment, so I quit and built my own. I kind of flourished there a little bit, but there was going to be a cap on it. Then I just didn't like the energy of the facility. But it always comes down to "create your own." You know what I mean? Nobody's going to take you seriously—somebody will! I feel like you almost have to put yourself forward, and a lot of times you are more ready than you realize or you get ready quicker. Your growth is accelerated if you are really focused on getting certain things done because you have to fend for yourself. So I say, create your own! That's what it comes down to.

Kallie Marie: So that's how we can combat that, yeah. What other types of entry barriers do you think women face, aside from not being taken seriously? Is there anything else?

Abhita Austin: [Laughs] Not being taken seriously . . . You know, Ebonie, she brought this to my attention. There's safety issues. Being in a dark, closed studio late at night, with all men. I never—I guess it's a blessing. I've never been in the situation where I feared for my life or was scared or aware of it. I didn't think anything of it. That is not, in a way, welcoming or smart, in a sense, if you are thinking safety-wise, [a] position for women to be in. I remember another artist brought that to my attention. She was just happy that I was a woman engineer. She just came to the session with these other guys, but she was just happy because she's had bad experiences. She doesn't like to be alone in the studio with men. I never—but that's so real.

Kallie Marie: Talk about extra cognitive load, to be thinking about that, to be safe while working . . .

Abhita Austin: That's crazy. And thank God, for whatever reason, I never felt scared. Like, my Spidey senses never—they went off once, I remember, and I was just like, "I will never do that again." It was like, somebody's basement studio. It was during the day, no windows, and I was just like, "It's real quiet in this place; what's going on?" My Spidey senses went off, and I was like, "Never again in my life."

I guess not being taken seriously has a lot of things under the fold that come under that category. But you know, I am not thinking of all the things right now. There's several barriers. But I guess that stereotype-threat thinking and also feeling within yourself when you are in those spaces that it's not inclusive—I guess on one level you get used to it, but then there's on another level, it's just like, "This is not a completely comfortable situation." It can take a toll on you.

Then under the category of not being taken seriously is sexual harassment, because that shit happens, I'm sure, to everybody. It happened to me before. I had to turn down work; I had to quit because of that. It's most unfortunate, because it directly connects to our pockets. I've had people try to holler at me during the session. So, to me, the unfortunate part about that is that as the engineer you are the ringleader; you are setting the tone, trying to make sure that everybody feels comfortable. You're trying to be welcoming. And when you get *that* in return, you're like, "Okay?" You still have to do it with a smile on your face. You kind of have to laugh it off and put the person in their line without offending them. To me, I know I have to do it; it has to be done. But in the back of my head I am thinking, "Why in the hell do I have to do this? It's wack that I have to smile in the face of this." But again, you have to be the bigger person.

To me, that bothers me. Like, why do I have to do that? Why am I put in this position? I've had studio owners, when I told them that, they don't get it. So that, in some cases, like the one particular case, I told them about this one artist, "Don't ever put me on a session with them," and they put me on the session with them later down the line, with him, because they needed the money. And it's just like, "Ohh no-nonono. You don't get it." You know these people have daughters. I don't understand what's going to . . . they're going to get it one way or the other. So yeah . . . You gotta do what you've gotta do.

Johnette Napolitano: I don't agree. If they weren't taken seriously in the first place, they wouldn't become established.

Kerry Pompeo: It's very important to not fall into the stereotypes of what a woman groupie could be or why you're there—because you want to hang out with the rock and roll guys or you are going to be there for eye candy. And it's a fine line, because you still want to be yourself, and that experience of me wearing T-shirts and jeans, a turtleneck because I didn't want to be overly sexualized. So, part of it, like, going out and networking, is just to have a tough skin, and it's really important to keep it professional. Like, it wouldn't fly in any other business, but because it's the music industry, we think that we have a cocktail in our hands, we think that there's no rules. But I was always just very professional and treated it like how business was supposed to be. Which meant doing my research so when I went to a networking event I knew what to talk about while I was there. Doing my research so I knew who I wanted to talk to because I always went into it like, I'm not even going to waste my time with the dudes that are here that are just "see a chick and want to prey on her." No, I am going to go to a source. So I always thought that it was really important: have a mission and to keep your eye on the prize because that's the only way you're going to get forward and get ahead. Again, it's the music business, and there's a lot of fun aspects on it that you can get lost on—and even easier because we are women.

It's just important to not be flattered if people are giving you flattery for anything else other than being an engineer. Shoot that shit down, because it's not why you are there in the first place. You know? If it's like, "You look good, girl," or something like that. You know what, you don't have to be bitchy about it; just deflect. Just be like, "Oh thanks, but I do not look as good as the microphone that we are looking at . . ." Turn it and spin it into a technical question because (a) they are not going to expect it, and (b) they will respect it, because then you're not like, "Oh, thank you for the compliment because you noticed my shoes" or something. No. Then, at that point, you're opening up a dialogue for you to talk about that.

So—and I have tons of tactics like that, because it's just years of doing it. I don't even realize I am doing it, but it's important. You always have a backup plan. You always have to educate yourself before walking into anything. Do your research, and that's that. And when you are doing research, you have to ask less questions, because you know the answers already. So the questions that you're asking are going to be really pointed that people will respect you for asking, rather than just being like, "What's the threshold knob do?" You're an engineer; you should fucking know that.

> **Kallie Marie:** Absolutely. It will be helpful for other women to hear what other people's tactics are, but I think the point is for people to be aware of the fact that we have to have tactics. Hopefully we will get to a place where we don't need tactics—that we can just walk into a room and just be people and get on with our profession and be excited about gear together instead of having to worry about people being focused on other things.

Andrea Yankovsky: There are a ton of entry barriers, starting with some of the math and science technology exposure, to what society tells us as women, how we are educated, combined with some mentorship issues. There's so much. And, again, it's so much of an individual thing too of someone's experience. And I think, actually, going back to the question of women helping other women, is a really big issue, that I think becomes a huge focus in a way that, to affect change, but also being careful that we don't cross the line into "separate but equal."

> **Kallie Marie:** That is something that I am very concerned with in this, because I don't want to be separate at all. I think that a lot of women are getting frustrated with that right now without having the vocabulary to articulate it. There are a lot of great networking

groups coming up for women in audio, but some women, to some extent, are worried that it will separate us. So we have to develop our vocabulary around these topics so that we are able to communicate effectively. It is not "separate but equal" but rather "closing the gap," as it were.

Andrea Yankovsky: Going back to—some people's minds are never going to change, but the more that women can advance the discussion and put it out there, and the more that people are just cognizant, just that little bit of it too. It's a process.

Anonymous: Women need to just start calling themselves producers and engineers and start producing content on their own or with friends without regard to outside validation. It is always going to be more challenging than for men, because if a man says he is a producer, likely everyone will believe it. But if a woman says she is a producer, there will likely be doubts in people's minds because they don't have enough examples of that being true.

I think stereotypically men will say they know how to do something even if they don't, and women try to be more truthful about their skills and experience, which ends up holding them back. I hate to admit that I've had to pump myself up before walking into certain nerve-wracking jobs by saying, "Think like a man," and wrangling my confidence. I saw many female counterparts shy away from work because they didn't think they were ready or good enough, and I just forced myself to say yes to jobs even when I wasn't sure I could do it or it made me nervous, then did my homework and read manuals or whatever I needed to do to get the job done well. Every time I got through a scary situation, I kept the experience in my back pocket as a reminder the next time I got intimidated. So I think, in general, women who want to succeed in this business have to stop analyzing their abilities so much and just prepare themselves and jump into the fire.

In terms of other entry barriers, I think little things like the way clothes are designed for women, not having as many pockets or belt loops or being as friendly for work. Also the assumption that as a woman you're still going to cook and take care of a house when it is really hard to do so with the long, late hours we work. And of course the fact that you have to convince other people that you are the engineer or producer and not someone's girlfriend or assistant.

Women are sometimes subconsciously or consciously excluded by a "boys' club" mentality in networking situations. What are some of your experiences with this? What impact did it have on you? What are some of the ways that this can be changed?

Leslie M. G. Bird: "Don't treat me like I'm invisible." That's what I wanted to say. I've had times where I was trying to implement some new technology and I was friendly with the person who is representing the company, and somebody would imply that I should sleep with him, being a woman. I know a lot of women who drink beer and put up with the club, but what are my experiences mentally?

Hillary Johnson: Oh, 100 percent.

Kallie Marie: What kind of effect did that have on you?

Hillary Johnson: I don't know. I've always been in the boys' club. I never liked the girls' club. I didn't care about Barbies or doing my hair. I was always a tomboy, so the boys' club has always been more comfortable for me anyway. Did I experience it? How did it affect me? I thought it was awesome! I liked talking about girls' butt, and rock 'n' roll and whatever when I was starting out, so I liked it. The fact that, again, because I was a person in somewhat a position of quote, unquote, "power," to use that word again, where I was the one charging them what I was charging them and booking them when I needed to book them, they were nice to me; they let me be in the boys' club. But also because it seemed like I was comfortable there; I wasn't trying to be something I wasn't.

I think the boys' club is only a problem for a woman who tries— either tries to be in the boys' club but doesn't really belong there or fights it. The boys' club isn't going away. It's always going to be there. Just like the girls' club is always going to be there. It's just when there's more boys, the boys' club seems obnoxious; when there's more girls, the girls' club seems obnoxious. There's no place for either of those things in the studio, but somehow the boys' club weaseled its way in. The girls are not—we don't care enough to stand up, to fight it, because we are like, "Whatever! Just shut up! Let's make records!"

Johnette Napolitano: Why should it be changed? I was in a band with two men for thirty years. They're my brothers. What, am I supposed to want it to be *The View*?

Andrea Yankovsky: Yes, because, how do you say this . . . Sometimes I wouldn't even call it the "boys' club." I would call it "cool kids' club," and what it takes to be cool . . . it's different for a woman versus a man. So I would say it's more like, it goes back to cliques; it goes back to high school. [Laughs] So that's one of the hard things, just even being different, in general. Whether it's your gender or whether it's something else, that can be tough.

Kallie Marie: Even if you just look at the aspects of drinking culture and networking and trying to deal with the gender differences as far as not being able to drink as much because I am smaller or the vulnerability that I then put myself in by being inebriated, and trying to manage a work environment, but in order to be "cool" I need to be hanging out and drinking . . .

Andrea Yankovsky: Yeah! Or there's the difference of people, if you get into intense conversations with somebody, and for me, I'm an intense person. [Laughs] So, I mean, if anybody . . . if I do that with a guy, people are like, "Hey, what's going on?" It's like, "Nothing!" [Laughs] Whereas if I am doing that with another woman, people are not going to make assumptions. If two guys are doing that, they're not going to make assumptions. You know, it's totally interesting too in terms of, I haven't been paying attention to how prevalent the rest of it has been when it comes to gay men in the music industry. In genres of music I know of, that there's more represented in certain genres—Broadway, or something . . . and what their experiences are?

Kallie Marie: Do you have any thoughts on how the networking conundrum can be changed?

Andrea Yankovsky: I think it comes with more women . . . More women, and, at the end of the day, there's always going to be some sort of boys' club to the extent that, going back to who's invited to the after-party. It's the cool kids, and that's how I think of it—"the cool kids' club." I think the more we get women in leadership positions, in prominent positions, in role models, that's where we're getting change. I think sometimes we just have to, by their nature, some of these institutional sexism issues, some of it is just basics of how people are. The society may not change, but the business may change in terms of—Who knows? Who am I to say that this will eventually become female-dominated, you know? I don't know! So the more women in it, the more women will be talking, and the other part of this, we are talking about all the problems, but there are a lot of really great men out there in the industry, and I don't want to make light of that. They need to be reinforced for them.

It's funny because, even what women need to do to help them-selves—and that's another big thing, sometimes leveraging the fact that you're a woman when a male engineer did something, went out of his way to really help me, and I sent him a thank-you note. Okay, most guys don't send thank-you notes. Most people don't even send hand-written things anymore. And his response was, "Wow, that's the nicest thing that anyone's done." But they were touched by that. It's like, as women we are taught, this is where the optimist part of me comes in, because at the end [of the] day, and I know I've said this to you before, it's all about relationships. That's something that women tend to be, as a more generalization, we are good at. We are more relationship-oriented.

Kallie Marie: We are certainly taught that.

Andrea Yankovsky: Yeah, exactly. I'm not saying inherently or what-ever, but whatever the cause of that is the result is that, we can use that to help us, help ourselves, because one of the other things that I was thinking a lot about recently was, right now, I am working on seeing that there's a group of people that have problems that I'm trying to craft a solution for. Realizing it's about the relationship, it's about them, it's not about me. That's another interesting thing too. 'Cause I was looking at—when you look at some of the websites, in my women en-trepreneurs group, when they were talking about Web design and who does—What does your website do? Who does it speak to? It's so funny, because you go on so many people's websites in the music industry, especially where it's just, like, "More me! Look at how fucking great I am!" and it's interesting because there, if you turn that around, and say, "Well what's this website supposed to do?" It's supposed to market yourself to potential clients. The website should really be about them, right? It's not about you. That just totally cracks me up, because I've learned that from talking to other women that get that, they get that faster, and they can implement that.

Anonymous: I've felt the "boys' club" mentality in work situations but not so much for networking. In terms of networking, I feel I've been invited and welcomed to events. But sometimes it can feel like too much if people put too much emphasis on "Wow, you're a female sound engineer."

Definitely guys will work together and help each other out more and hook each other up with jobs even if a guy doesn't have much experience, but maybe because he's stronger or more vocal. I think that's the key, though—just making a lot of noise, reminding people that you're around, and speaking up if you want something and owning what you want.

The whole Recording Academy at times feels like a White boys' club—for example, only one Grammy category for all of world music. I also had an issue when I signed up; they had on my profile that I was an "assistant engineer" when none of the credits I had submitted for voting status had been as an assistant. They had all been as the recording or mixing engineer. When I asked them about it, they changed my job title to "Other." When I complained about that, they took the job line off altogether and never followed up with me. It was also unclear if I was ever included in the Engineer and Producers Wing. I've heard they're trying to diversify and want more women and people of color, but I can't say I honestly see them working toward that.

CULTURAL BACKLASH AND PAY EQUITY

In the past, certain technical industries, like computing, initially had high numbers of women working in the field but at lower wages. Then, once more men entered the field, wages increased, and women began to be excluded. As more women enter audio engineering and music production, there may be a risk of backlash and in turn a risk to current industry wages. What can be done to ensure that this doesn't occur? What issues have you experienced with pay equity?

Abhita Austin: Most of my label experience has been as an engineer, and I don't know if it was related to me being a woman, but sometimes I would have to, you know, chase people to get paid. I literally rolled up to a record company and had to, and these are people, I am dealing with like A&R gatekeepers, so they would hire me for the session, I would think I am getting paid because I invoiced and got the PO number, and then the money would not come. Weeks, months would go by, so I would have to consistently call, roll up on the offices, and chase whoever down and find the person in finance and make sure they cut the check. So, would that have happened if I was a man? I don't know. Would they have tried it? I am not sure. I also noticed an element: the stature of a man will affect the male gatekeeper. You know, I have heard of managers who look like bouncers, and that's one of their assets, where they are going to make whoever that male gatekeeper is move to whatever the artist needs. I feel like that's an experience I have had of pushback—the situation I have had of them pushing back on my money. Some cases I never got paid! Chase, chase, chase and never got paid. There's still some artists that have never gotten paid . . .

I would be guessing, I don't know. I think that, one, the industry is changing so much, I don't even know what the wages are at this point. Like, is there a studio? There's, like, five? Jungle City in New York and a couple others. I think Right Track is still there? Some form of Right Track? I think that the studio across the street—I was just at it, starts with a P? Because we did a shoot there at it; I forgot the name of it—it just closed last summer. It closed. One of the women who were at Gender Amplified, she used to work there, and that closed. So, I mean, how many studios are there? But I don't know. I don't even know what the wages are.

But backlash, backlash on more women? I think we are so far off from 20 percent [of women in the industry]. What are we at, a 5 percent? Maybe 4 percent?

Kallie Marie: The statistic I have heard is 95 percent of audio engineers and music producers are men. We have 5 percent, and we only have 2 percent of film composers that are women.

Abhita Austin: Wow, wow. And you think of it, like—and the only thing that I can think is that, "Why is that the case?" I know it's not a question, but, like, I remember I was like, "Oh, I have no idea." I think it's not just that women aren't encouraged to be in a technical field; they're discouraged once they are in there. I think that's the big factor. People don't want to, or at least men don't want to, be aware of.

Kallie Marie: What does that discouragement look like?

Abhita Austin: It looks like being shifted into a role of manager or somebody at the front desk. It looks like being told you're not an engineer. It looks like being sexually harassed. It looks like being put in these unsafe spaces. It looks like a whole bunch of things. It looks like hanging out in a male locker room, which is like, "What the hell is going on here?" I remember that was life shifting when I was hearing what they were talking about. I was like, "What is going on??" Craziness! It's just amazing.

Kallie Marie: We need to highlight what these things are, because the men that do care, that are interested in inclusiveness, that do want things to change—this helps, these visibilities, for them to know what the issues even are. Because these things can be so small that they are not going to experience them. So somebody needs to highlight them so that they can be seen. Too often the response is, "Oh, that had never occurred to me that that might happen, that that might be a problem, because I've never seen it." Which is often, I think, the pushback that is experienced, is that, "Well, I've never noticed that, so it can't be true."

Abhita Austin: What I am hearing now is pleasing me, is that I have heard some men say, musicians in particular, that actually ask me about some—but I don't know how it got onto the conversation about sexual harassment, because they were like, "I know it happens; I have seen it." And I was like, "Wow." That's new to me. I guess this is coming from the younger generation. I think they are more—I think the Internet brings more awareness to various issues. I think people are thinking a little bit more actively, and I would say men are thinking a little bit more openly about it and becoming more aware. But I think you are right: the people who have some type of vision and understand and are the men who get it or want to be aware, it's good to let them know.

Kallie Marie: Especially the men that are in positions of power. They can change things. The ones who are not coming up with the younger generations, who have been where they are for a while, who've watched many things happen in the industry. Now there's this, and if they're up for helping, then I think we have certainly got to let them know *how*. That's an opportunity to be taken.

Abhita Austin: For sure. I feel like also it's important on your daily path to correct folks when you hear craziness, and I think it takes a certain amount of courage to do it. And you definitely don't want to put yourself in a position where you won't have a job, so I would not recommend, like, doing it in a session if it's gonna jack you up or whatever financially, but as much as you can to let people know.

"There's another opinion" or "What they are saying is kinda crazy"—I think that's important.

Leslie M. G. Bird: I don't think we can always say, "Hey, this is this," from my role. I'm just starting to see women. I work my ass off looking to hire extra women. I work just as hard as them, so, yeah . . . Let it happen. I think just be clear what our mission is.

> **Kallie Marie:** To follow up, I wonder sometimes because people will get pushback about not hiring on merit anymore and that suggests that women aren't as good, so it does open a can of worms. In that regard, I think it makes some men angry because they feel they are being passed over in favor of someone who is inferior. And so, again, we have to look at these types of nuances in order to present things the right way. Do you have any thoughts on that?

> **Leslie M. G. Bird:** Yeah. I think in my role, advocating for changes in the industry, we're really being careful to construct a strong message, and that's why I have to have committees, and that's why I have to have diversity committees, and that's why I hope to have people who see the need for it. Because I'll tell you that everybody's on the diversity-inclusion bandwagon. When I do this work, I'm always saying, "Look, here's our proposal. Do you see problems with this language? So we all agree, right?" Everybody needs to be on the same page, because if you are by yourself, then they can just shut you up and put the pressure on. The weight of an entire international voice changes—absolutely. Absolutely.

> **Kallie Marie:** So tagging on from this, this conversation, have you experienced any issues with pay equity?

> **Leslie M. G. Bird:** Oh, that's a hard thing to talk about in a book interview, especially when you are litigating. I think I have to leave it right there. How about: Yes.

Hillary Johnson: No, I don't think so. I think that we've done a good enough job at demeaning ourselves by making it possible for artists to make records on their computers. I think we've done it to ourselves already. I don't think that anything will change with having more women in the industry.

There've always been women in television production and film and things like that, so I don't think that that will change. I think that it's only a sort of a nongendered issue if the overall sort of rates of what people are getting paid goes down. I [sometimes] think, "Having women [could] help?" But I doubt it—I don't think so. I don't think it makes a difference.

Kallie Marie: Have you ever experienced any pay-equity issues or anything like that?

Hillary Johnson: I don't think so. I know there's plenty of boys I make more than—not because I am a woman, though, but just because I know more, because of experience. No, I think I've always been paid the same as my coworkers in anything I've done, if that person is my peer, you know?

Sylvia Massy: I'm not sure that that's going to happen. It's such a specific type of job. I haven't felt any discrimination as far as wages because I am a woman, but then there's not that many women doing it, so . . . Yeah, I think that the more experience they have, it's kind of like, "What have you done lately?" Like, you look at someone like Linda Perry, who is a producer who's worked with Pink and Christina Aguilera; she gets paid top dollar because she has the track record to prove that she's worth it. So I think, if you have the track record, you're going to demand the type of wages. I can't say there's a discrimination.

I don't see that happening. At this point, wages are coming down but only because of the availability of the equipment. So that's more what is driving the wages. And, yes, the wages are coming down. For instance, mixing work—you can get a mixer for a quarter of the price of ten years ago now just because of the availability of the equipment. So I don't see that particular dynamic happening with engineering.

Johnette Napolitano: That's a bigger social issue than appropriate in this context. The entertainment industry is no different than any other industry in the face of economic crisis and, in fact, always do better during depression.

I've always thought that so egotistical: the whole country is not New York, California, LA.

"Never equate your paycheck with your talent"—Marlon Brando. In other words, there are no rules, and pay scales depend on a lot of different things.

Kerry Pompeo: Well, getting paid, in general . . . coming up . . . I think it's more like an engineering, not gender-specific. When you are up-and-coming in this industry, that can be an issue—getting paid. It's not like other businesses where you work for free. You're not going to go to the grocery store and say, "Can I pay you next week for this? . . ."

> **Kallie Marie:** I use the haircut analogy all the time: "Cut my hair, let me see if I like it. If I like it, you know you're going to get lots of exposure, because people are going to ask me where I got it done, but, you know, you've never cut my hair before, so I don't know if I am going to like it. How about I just see how it goes, and then I'll tell everyone you did it, and that will get you more work?"

Kerry Pompeo: You know how many times that people tried that line on me? Maybe women would be more susceptible to that because they feel like they have to prove themselves more?

Kallie Marie: That's interesting. I didn't think of that . . .

Kerry Pompeo: So, I think that—and again it's a confidence thing—[you] just have to be comfortable with saying no to those people. Just walk away. Or it has to be something. You can't have something for nothing. Like, "No, dude. Exposure??" . . . This isn't a hobby for me, and a lot of people think that because, oh, I'm smiling while I am working, then it's fun; and, yeah it's fun, but this is how I put food on the table.

Kallie Marie: Yes, and I think that's shared by everybody in this business.

Kerry Pompeo: But as far as, like, equity, that's interesting, because I think a lot of us, because there's no studio hierarchy, a lot of us are independent, so it's what we deem we are worth. So I think that can come into play. I'm in a situation where I am working for a big company, so I haven't been here long enough to say if it is a factor, because I am the only one that's new, so there's a seniority thing, but I am also the only one that's a woman. So, again, you have to see the seniority. But if somebody's here the same amount of time that I am . . . and is a man that gets paid more, then that's messed up!

As far as "Do I ever think that if there was enough of us in this business, it would be considered women's work?" I think that would be fucking awesome! "Oh, shit—give her a chick job. Make her the head engineer!"

Kallie Marie: I am looking ahead at any potential backlash that we might face, as there is historical precedent for that occurring, and if there is anything that anyone could spot out, what we should be looking out for coming ahead. Perhaps it's too far ahead?

Kerry Pompeo: On *Orange Is the New Black*, there's a scene where Boo, she's like, "Oh, of course the big dike does the stagehand role!" And you know, I think certain stereotypes—if women are going to be working in the stage business, then they have to be really strong. I think it's a stereotype, and I don't know if that's backlash, but even when women are included, we are stereotyped.

I used to push fucking Hammond organs around—like, big fucking B3s. So I worked extra hard! That's why I was pushing that Hammond around—because I knew that they didn't think I could do it, so I did it. But that only adds moral fiber, I think.

> **Kallie Marie:** It would be nice if the perception could be that women are strong. Not every human is strong. There are plenty of men with back problems, women, too. People can look strong and big, but they could have a variety of health issues or injuries. The fact that we are having this conversation about how we tactically have pushed and lifted gear to show off and flex . . . because if we don't, then suddenly someone might put you in a different box, and we are trying to prevent that box, and that's its own thing in and of itself.

Andrea Yankovsky: That's a really good question. I would speculate potentially that risk, but I also feel like there is a lot of women that can do for themselves. While we face—there's sort of a dialectic there in that we didn't cause these problems but we have to deal with them. Guess what? For the most part, no one's going to deal with them for you. [Laughs] So, I don't mean to take responsibility off of the industry, off of society, all of the sort of things. Don't get me wrong there. But it also means that you as an individual have to figure out how to navigate it. I was talking—I had a conversation the other day about negotiations. I tell you what, negotiations about money, negotiations about rights and all that sort of stuff—those are difficult conversations. I mean, you've seen, there's gender issues when it comes to that sort of thing, power dynamics and all of that. And so, really, seeing where—and this is where women can help themselves—is seeing where they might have a weakness or there's an area that they can improve to help their own cause, help their own position, that is also in line with, and is authentic for them, and in line with who they are, what they want to do, and who they want to be. So then I think that's huge. So, if women build skills in those areas, I think that the industry would be less susceptible to a wage gap. If we arm ourselves with the skills to negotiate deals and we also don't sell ourselves short, that's powerful.

Anonymous: As far as I know, I've been paid equally as my male counterparts. People have to demand better wages and not work for less by realizing that it will bring everyone's rate down.

STUDIO MOM AND THE RELEGATION OF ALL THINGS "GLORIFIED SECRETARIAL"

It is highly prevalent in our culture for women in the workplace to be relegated to things akin to domestic tasks and hospitality—remembering office birthdays, bringing food for office parties, being on the front lines of hospitality, et cetera. In what ways is this experienced in the recording studio?

Johnette Napolitano: I love doing that—really love it. Makes me feel like home. Always decorating the bus, cleaning up. I really need that for myself.

PROBLEMATIC QUESTIONS IN JOURNALISM: CHANGING THE CONVERSATION

A common question for women in music production often asked by journalists is how they may have chosen to produce other women. How are questions like this part of a larger attitude toward female producers? How are these types of questions problematic? For example, are men asked if they chose to work with other men? How are women unintentionally set apart by asking these types of questions in interviews? What types of questions are becoming outdated? How can the conversation be changed in order to move forward?

Abhita Austin: It's problematic because it's coming from a sexist gaze, from, like, a place of not even respecting the woman producer's actual craft. They are really just focusing in on her gender. We are focused—in general, we are talking about women in production because they're separate, for the lack of us. On the flip side, it comes back to that thing of not being taken seriously. Why would you even—it's such a, I don't want to say, "dumb," but it's not a smart question. It comes from someone who is not focused on the right things, which is the music and the woman's craft. It comes from somebody who is . . . sexist. That's pretty much it. It could be a woman asking or it could be a man.

> **Kallie Marie:** How are women unintentionally or intentionally set apart by asking these types of questions in interviews? What types of questions are becoming outdated? What should we not be asking women in music production when we get an interview with them? What are the outdated questions? What do we need to move on from? How do we move the conversation forward?

Abhita Austin: Maybe if you're interviewing a woman—well, it's tricky. Like I said, you have to be aware. Like, you can't just completely ignore that there's a bias, and I see a lot of people who do that, and I think that they are trying to compensate. They are trying to move past it, like you were saying. But I just feel like not steering the conversation completely that direction. If you are doing ten questions, maybe one or two can be around that, the discrimination around women being producers or the lack of women producers. But, like, I would find it more interesting if you spoke about the creative process or just regular questions that you would ask! How they got started, their philosophy around production . . . It's not to me, if you're interviewing somebody, it's so much more than just them being a woman producer. Again, I think, if they are focused just on that, it's a different mindset. It can be problematic. It's the questions being asked, and it's the light being flashed. It's actually seeing the woman doing the work.

Hillary Johnson: I don't necessarily think so. I don't think it's a bad thing that the journalists are trying to find an angle to an age-old story. I think that if there's any kind of press for women in our industry, I think it's good press. If the interviewer is only asking about the records or whatever that that person has done with female artists, then there might be a problem, but then it's—you would think that naturally the answers would happen where it should shift topics.

> **Kallie Marie:** I was thinking about this phenomenon, because when a man works with another man, people don't seem to question, "Oh, the two of you men working together in the studio." It's like, "Well, of course!"

Hillary Johnson: Yeah, there's all sorts of other little questions that journalists like to do, like, "Did you hang out with his wife?" or whatever.

> **Kallie Marie:** Right. Are there any types of questions that you feel that journalists should not be asking or should be asking women in interviews, specifically producers or engineers? Any kind of outdated questions that you think you know don't need to be asked anymore? What things do you think the conversation should be more geared toward?

Hillary Johnson: I think it depends. A normal industry-magazine interview is focusing on the fact that someone's female, working in this industry, I think a lot of those questions should be not asked. But if it's like this, a woman asking another woman, then I think there's nothing that shouldn't be asked. It's all sort of who's the audience, I guess.

> **Kallie Marie:** Absolutely. And because it is the reason why I am asking this, is again, it's about perception and presentation and visibility. So, if we are working on having women be perceived with the technical attributes and skills that we have, we [want] to show that, yes, women are technical, what kind of questions should we be asking women? I am hoping the answer is "The same questions that we ask men about gear!" so that people can really value our contributions, over just our sort of unicorn quality, instead of like, "Look—a unicorn!"

Hillary Johnson: The set of questions that I don't get asked enough is, "Why do you like the microphones you like? Why do you like the speakers you like? What do you do when you have phase problems with drums?" To go back to what I said earlier, I think that women need to be asked more technical-opinion questions. Rather than more questions of, "How did you get into this field?" I mean, it's different if someone is unknown and maybe has done something really niche or niche in their career. But if they are just making records, like any other dude making records, then you ask them how they got started, it's kind of an uneducated question. Versus a person who is writing for, maybe, a magazine, and maybe they're writing an article on compressors or something. So they are asking all these engineers all these things, and they ask a woman the same things—"What's the best ratio for vocal in a rock record?" not, you know, "So, did you have—did your dad support you growing up?" You know, so, I mean, it depends.

> **Kallie Marie:** Right. I think it is important to look at these kinds of aspects, because . . . the way we get presented in the press is important. It's significant because that's where people are going to gain exposure and whether—not just for women coming up, but that's

where people are going to hear about other women in their field. It's important to also see ourselves represented there.

Sylvia Massy: I guess just because I'm such an odd, rare bird, the question that comes up so often, which I'm, like, "C'mon, wow," is, "What's it like being a woman in a man's world?" And it's like, "Oh god, really? You're gonna ask me that question?" But I think that's entirely what we are talking about now, so I'm totally willing to answer the questions, but it's because my attitude about it is different than maybe some other people. I don't find that there's a big conspiracy against women in this field of work, so I think that most—that there's a lot of people that kind of expect me to say, "Yeah, these men are hurting women," and I just don't see it. I think it's difficult to get into this job for both men and women, and there's reasons why women don't get into it, and it has to do with biology, basically between men and women, what women perceive as the type of work that they want to do that will fulfill them for the rest of their life.

> **Kallie Marie:** Do you think that there's any questions that the press or the media should get over? That they should just stop asking women in music production? What are more productive questions or conversations that we could be having?

Sylvia Massy: Oh, yeah. I think that the biggest question for everybody right now is how any of us in engineering and production can continue to get paid for our work. Especially musicians. Musicians have the biggest challenge of all because they're not getting support from labels like they used to. Labels aren't able to make money like they used to. So the whole industry is kind of flopped on its back like a beetle with the feet in the air. It's like we haven't figured how to make it upright yet, where the bands get paid. When the bands get paid, then we all get paid. It used to be that taking a percentage of a project—say, I'll do work in exchange for a percentage of your profits on the tail end, points. That's not worth a whole lot anymore, unless you're working with Dave Matthews Band or something. Getting points on an album isn't really going to turn into a royalty that you can live on. So, yeah, the big question for all of us now, men and women, is "How are we going to make money with this anymore?" I think that I'm lucky that I got into it when I did and had some great successes and that will continue me working hopefully until the end of my days. But for the next generation of new people, there is a big question: "How is everyone going to make money when the bands don't make money?" That's the biggest question. That's the one we should be asking.

Andrea Yankovsky: The press can be part of the problem. I really found that sometimes I had to step outside and get other opinions. But step outside the music industry to bring some strength and knowledge, or whatever industry that I am working. Like, right now . . . the person who I'm looking to for guidance to help build my business has nothing to do with anything with any industry I have ever worked in. That's not what her experience is. But she has, accordingly, she has these ideas and solutions that haven't been implemented in the music industry or recording industry or whatever. Who was it? I remember, it may have been Nile Rodgers at one of the AES things that said—we were talking about creativity—"Creative people are always going to figure out creative solutions." One of our jobs as engineers is to find answers to problems, right? And use the tools that we have to make something happen. Sometimes, and we might have to go outside of our sphere. I think we've touched on this before, when we were talking about how people don't wanna have a conversation or, like, "Oh, enough diversity and stuff!" Like that . . . I think it was at an AES conference! [Laughs] I don't mean to bang on the AES. I love—there's so many people. It's just something that's more top-of-mind right now. I was having this conversation with someone at the AES conference a couple of years ago, and I think one of the seminars or discussions was like, "Chicks in Audio," or something like that. And I was like, "Okay, did anybody notice the title of your seminar? Hello??" [Laughs] I'm not so much a stickler for semantics words and stuff like that, but that one was a little belligerent.

Anonymous: I think it goes back to the above response about art being made by women getting all lumped into its own category or genre. I think it's important to talk about gender issues and expose the everyday sexism. But in general I've found that, the longer I'm doing this, the less interested I am in talking about gender. At a certain point you get tired of talking about it, and you realize you can't really make generalizations about everyone. You can't ignore it, but it can't always be the focus also.

Questions about a woman's fashion choice would seem outdated if the interview is about music production. I think if an interviewer asked him/herself beforehand, "Would I ask these questions of a man?" that would be a good guide for whether they should ask a woman those questions.

6

CLOSING REMARKS

Awareness and the Future

Earlier in the book we asked, "When is there more than one woman?"—an evaluation on the impact of singularity and lack of collaborative representation and visibility. I later asked interviewees about their experiences producing and engineering women artists (rather than working alongside them as second engineers, producers, assistant engineers, and so on) and if they had any reflections on this work or if they had any insights regarding their experiences. I was curious about how they'd come to these opportunities to work with women artists, if at all. Strikingly, some may be surprised to find that the majority of musicians they worked with—either recording or producing—were male as well, barring the role of singers. So women seeing each other on either side of the glass is rare in most instances, depending on the genre of music and sometimes the instrument.

The experience for the artist of having a woman as an engineer or producer may also have an impact on the artist and their creative output. This first came to my mind in 2008 while I was working at a large recording studio in New York City. A vocalist arrived to record by herself, and there were three of us on the team that day, two men and myself. The next time she returned to the studio, she left a thank-you note for me, saying how comforted she was to have another woman in the room. She didn't elaborate on why, but it was understood. If we are overlooking women's experiences as artists during the recording process, it will definitely have an impact on the music being made.

I wondered how the interviewees viewed the times they had worked with other women as artists. How was it a different experience from having worked with other women who were engineers or producers on their team? Some said the dynamic was a lot of fun. Some felt the artists reached out, saying they felt safer or felt it was easier to establish trust. Some of the people interviewed here have names that are Grammy-adjacent and will have had an entirely different experience with why an artist might choose to work with them. For others there were different interpretations about their experiences.

In closing, I asked each of the women if they had anything they wanted to share or raise awareness about. After all the questions and complex topics I wondered if there was anything I may have missed, anything they wanted to voice, or if they had thoughts they wanted to share about the future. It's important as we look forward to the future to not only establish goals but have solutions and the vocabulary to articulate the why and how of the progress we seek. Curating a conversation of this nature allowed a unique opportunity to discuss success, struggles, and the future potential for collective, continued progress.

Here are the women's closing thoughts on the discussion.

BEING APPROACHED BY WOMEN ARTISTS: WHY DO THEY SEEK OUT WOMEN ENGINEERS AND PRODUCERS? EXPERIENCES AND REFLECTIONS

When women artists specifically seek out a female producer, what has been the reason behind it, in your experience?

Johnette Napolitano: I haven't the foggiest. If I were to seek out a producer, it would be because I liked a record enough to bother to find out who was involved.

Anonymous: In my experience, some women want to help promote other women in art and music, so it's a way of elevating each other. Also, some women may feel more comfortable with another woman and intimidated sharing their ideas with a man. Or they're wary of male producers with ulterior motives, so they know with a woman there's likely not going to be some awkward sexual tension or be put on the spot sexually or romantically.

SHARED STORIES, RAISING AWARENESS, AND CLOSING REMARKS ABOUT THE FUTURE

In the interest of raising awareness, do you have any instances, obstacles, or stories that you think people would be surprised to hear about? Or an obstacle that you haven't personally experienced but know of through other women? Are there any subtle but consistent barriers that persist that you would like to raise awareness about?

Abhita Austin: I don't know if people would be surprised, but like I mentioned before, I had to quit because of sexual harassment. Because, basically, the manager was not willing to honor what I asked for. Unbelievable.

I can't think of anything off the top of my head.

Leslie M. G. Bird: True story I want to tell that surprised even myself. WAM had a Christmas party, and I was sitting in the control room, right? And I don't remember, I have never in my life [at a] listening [party heard] two women on speakers. To be a guy, you know how many listening parties you have been in and it's the guys? It gave me chills. I think that experience should not be relegated to San Francisco, you know? I haven't seen any situations like that ever happen anywhere else, and it's a shame. It's just that it's so powerful. I just—I just wanted to say, "I love everybody in this room," and I'm not even allowed. I mean, I'm assuming is by necessity and I'm a woman, but, you know, if I could be proud to be like the pagans going barefoot in the woods, I would do that too. But just, like, holy shit this being freaking pagan experience! Do you know what I mean? So, you know, I just wanted to love those women, and coming back to Denver and not having anything like that, I mean, we have our little group of five or six women who get happy hours. Any little thing creating an experience and more than what I'm doing. I'm happy to be included in your book, and if there's anything else I can do for the next engineering book or whatever, just let me know. This is the different degrees, like for Terri and Kerry and Anthony, and for you I'm sure it is a life calling.

Hillary Johnson: Well, for years, and probably still to a certain extent, it's not that I fought against being represented as a woman, a female engineer, but I kind of tried to shy away from it, because I felt that [it] was not helping me. I felt that by people focusing on the fact that I was a woman doing this was actually taking away from any credibility. And so, this is how I have felt for years and only recently thought, "Maybe I should have been using this to my advantage?" But I haven't come to any conclusion yet, and that's just sort of where I am now, and that maybe I should be sort of flaunting the fact that there's not a lot of women and I am one and this is what I do and I have a lot of experience. Maybe it will get me more exposure. Maybe I will be able to make more records that I want to make. I don't know. It's a popularity contest; it's all a popularity contest. It's who you know, who've you worked with and if you know—and I'm not competitive. I mean, I *am* competitive, but I'm not like—I don't go seek out things and try and get records. I am too old for that. So, you know, so maybe if I just stopped fighting the fact that I was a woman earlier on it would have made me a little more popular, and it would have put my name out there more, and I would have had more of a name, and I would have been actually more quote, unquote, "successful." I mean, I feel pretty happy with my career, so it's relative, but I've told a couple people that recently, and they were kind of surprised by that. So there's your surprise.

Johnette Napolitano: Things are so different now than when I started. I think it would be an entirely different perspective. I'm blown away every day at the fresh young art on the Internet—so much going on. Who even knows what sex anyone is? Very interesting times.

Kerry Pompeo: If I can offer one anecdote of something fucked-up that did happen to me, and it was really the only thing that happened, was I was [an] engineer at studio where we had a large analogue console and lots of patch bays and everything, and I worked close by—like, to the point where we would go home if problems happened. People would call me in to solve the issue. And these mysterious things kept happening with the patch bay. So I go over and plug it in—I have to reach over and plug it in, like, reconfigure everything. And like, "Oh, you know, something's not right." Things would be moved around, and I had to go back there and repatch things all over again. Turns out, the dudes were pulling things out and screwing it up so that they could have me come back in the room and bend over and fix all the patches! So after this happened like three times, I kind of got hip to it, because I look over my shoulder and realized, and I'm not wearing a dress, I am wearing jeans or whatever, I'm not in a short skirt, not that that should even be a problem, but when I got wind and I looked over my shoulder and I saw their smirks, and I think, like, they said something, because I was like, "I knew I didn't patch those in there. And they were recording for like an hour, so why all the sudden is it all wrong?" So that was why. So I just took everything out, and I ripped all the patch cords, and I said, "Fix it if you want your session to go on. Go on, fix it yourself," because I had the control in the room. I pulled every single one of them out: "Now, what are you going to do? Have fun with the rest of your session." I was so fucking pissed—like, "Really??" They think . . . you're not smart enough to fix it. But, yeah. Just to have me come in . . . and I knew once I had ripped everything out they wouldn't be able to put it back together. So I ripped everything out because we have things [that] just always stay, like the monitors, the keypads, and things like that. They probably might have known how to patch a microphone in . . . through some gear, but . . . I knew where everything was, so I just ripped it all fucking out . . .

You know, and these were people that would work overnight all the time. So now you are here, you are just going to sit with your schlong in your hand and wish that you didn't do that, because I could have probably helped you. Or if you would have asked for my advice, I maybe would have sat in the room and told you that it really sounded shitty, what you were doing, and I could have twisted a couple of knobs instead . . . and made it better . . . So I don't think they are doing music anymore . . . So that's my story.

Ebonie Smith: This is something that I want to shed light on. I don't know if this . . . perfectly answers your question, but it's something that I want to shed light on. What happens when you're the person as a woman, when you're the person in control and you are the one who—how can I phrase this—this idea of romance in the studio business? Because so often the conversation is like, "What happens when the guy wants you and you don't want the guy?" "Well, what happens when you want the guy?" "What happens when you're in a position of wanting to explore romantically?" Because when you are making music with people, it's a very intimate time. I was listening to Chelsea Handler. Chelsea actually dated, like, the CEO of her network at one time or something. I was listening to an interview, and they asked her, like, "Don't you think it's a conflict of interest to date the CEO of your network, a top executive at your network?" and she was like, "No! You spend half your time at work. Like, who says you can't date somebody you work with? You spend half your time there. That's where you meet people you like, who are common-minded." I don't feel any kind of issues with that, and I thought that was a very interesting perspective. Because as a woman I'm meeting people in the studio that I am attracted to all the time. It's handling that. How do women handle that? It's easy to fall for somebody you are working with. When you are the person in power, you are in a position of influence, and the scale is tipped—or, rather, the circumstances are inverted. How do women deal with being attracted—women engineers and producers, women studio owners—being attracted to the men or the women who you are working with? How do women—with the stigma that's already there anyway, with the loneliness that could be your experience as a woman in audio—how do you negotiate that? Is it appropriate? It's more of a question for your question, but, like, it is something that I wanted to bring awareness to . . . this idea of romance and the studio and women being interested. Because so often it is the other way around. You know this guy is interested, in the studio, and how women deal with that type of aggression coming from men. It's like, it can be the other way around too. How do women negotiate falling in love when they make records or being attracted to clients or, you know, any of that type of things? Just wanted to bring that up.

Anonymous: I included several stories in responses above, but also . . . I was at Guitar Center—first mistake—years ago buying a new audio interface to replace my old one, and as I'm holding the box, a random sales guy walks by and asks, "Just starting to record?" At that point I was getting paid as a recording engineer in a couple different studios, but this guy assumed I was a beginner without even talking to me because of my anatomy. It is also not uncommon if I have a male assistant that the client or talent will approach the assistant first or assume he is the lead.

Getting the right credits can be challenging as well. There was an album I recorded drums and bass for, and my boyfriend at the time played in the band and co-produced the album with another band member. When it was finally finished and I looked at the album credits, I had a co-engineering credit, shared with my ex-boyfriend, because the other producer didn't want to share his producing credit. So I had worked for years to get the skills and experience to do the recordings all on my own and still had to share the credit with a guy who had no clue about recording and hadn't even touched a button. Again, women in this industry work twice as hard for the same recognition.

Wrapping up the interview, are there any thoughts you would like to add?

Abhita Austin: I feel like we went through so much. Just to reiterate, I feel like the key is creating your own path and being a leader in that. Setting yourself up as a leader in that path and being able to curate and craft it. Because I feel like there's no other way to—it's too hard of a battle to change somebody's consciousness around sexism. That is just something that they came up with; they were nurtured since they were probably born to think of women in a certain way. So I feel like, over time, if there are more channels and visibility of women—led by women who have an interest of highlighting women producers in a proper light—then I think that's going to bring the change. I'm not leaving it up to these guys. That's it!

Leslie M. G. Bird: Thank you for inviting me to be a part of this, because it's important work.

Hillary Johnson: No, I think just my only point that I would want to make sure comes across is, if any woman has any interest at all in any field within the music industry that they should just do it, go for it, learn it, and try their best to just ignore the crap that comes along with it, because to do the work and to not just assume that you're going to get everything handed to you because you care, because we all know that's not true. So just go for it. Do it. You want to do it, do it. Don't let anyone discourage you—you know, your parents, your friends, your partner, your competition. Because you won't be happy unless you just do what you want to do. That's definitely spoken from experience, for sure. I would be very unhappy if I had stopped doing anything that I do.

Johnette Napolitano: It's always about the music first. Make music for blind people. I'm always called "sir" over the phone, so, whatever.

Kerry Pompeo: Okay, so, I never—and I think it's pretty apparent, by the way I was attacking the questions—that I never let my gender be even thought about, even as myself in the studio, because I didn't think it had a place. It's like, we're not men/women; we're here, and we're professionals. We are artists. Let's get it done. I think through having that confidence, it translated to people. I never really had anybody say to my face anything that they felt that I was inadequate, but I've had a lot of people tell me that they thought it was really cool that a girl was working and twisted the knobs and knew more than they did. People have given me a really positive attitude. I think part of it is because I walked in and even if I didn't know everything, I acted like I did. You just want to have people feel secure, like you're driving the ship. So I always made it understood that I am driving the ship; you're walking into my thing. Even as when you are coming up as an assistant, letting people know [you know] where everything is in the studio. Making people feel confident in you and putting—you know, if a guitar player has got his, you know, guitar slummed on a chair, putting [it] on a rack for him or a stand for him or her—see? I am doing it—for *them*, while putting it on a stand for them, or . . . just basically letting people know that this is your domain. I think it helps. People always liked that I broke up the vibe in the room, like, I broke up the all-men thing. They always said it's a refreshing perspective. Because I would hear things. I have a different perspective, so when I was coming up with comments or ideas, it was coming from a different place, and it was always appreciated. And I think that's really important for people to realize and not to feel like, "Oh, it's coming from a girl's place . . ." Why wouldn't they want it to come from more of an objective space? So I think that women need to feel that they should be in the studio, because we need it for projects, for art to be elevated and better. They need to feel, more importantly, that this is their place, because if that's not happening, then they are not going to feel comfortable, and they are not going to feel confident. It's a trickle-down. You need to feel like, "Girl, you own it!" But for real, that always worked for me. But, just [to] summarize, ask a question when it's in your heart, that you feel like you belong there, just do anything and everything to own it, and to be there and to be prepared for a very long journey. Because it's a long [one] regardless of your gender. And it might be a little bit longer, you might have to work a little bit harder, if times don't change, but I think they are changing very rapidly right now.

I think that there's a long enough way before that we would totally take everything over for there to be any backlash. To be an overall easy-to-work-with person, that's not a female thing. You have to have an open mind in this business, and you have to be able to take what people say, even if it's harsh, and be able to use it to be able to benefit from it or grow from it. I tell people all the time when I am working with them, "You can tell me whatever you want. My job is not to put my opinion on you; my job is to do what's right for the song. So I am going to tell you what I think, and I want you to tell me what you think." . . . Musicians and artists sometimes can't describe things technically, so sometimes things sound harsh, so you can't be really taken [back] by that. [You] kind of have to decipher what they mean, have thick skin. But that's just the music business.

AFTERWORD

Countless examples of women working in audio engineering and music production exist who have achieved high levels of success, and with that comes their years of lived experiences. In many cases, those experiences are shared experiences. For too long it has been supposed that maybe we don't see any women in these fields because they "aren't interested in it" or simply "aren't technical enough." There are enough women working, on record, and not just working but *succeeding* that the case can no longer be made that they don't exist, aren't interested, or aren't capable. Furthermore, as we better understand and improve early childhood development, diversify educational influences, increase exposure to STEAM subjects, foster opportunities that foster engagement, and encourage success, we should see a continued growth in the interest in the subject areas.

Interest is not enough, though. What happens to these people as they enter the professional world will be impacted by how they are mentored, how they are promoted, and the types of opportunities they are given. They must be allowed to experiment, fail, and grow their confidence, as we all should. Women and their professional contributions must be remembered correctly rather than misremembered and not deprofessionalized. Better and proper representation will help curb stereotype threat, and in time we may see a leveling of the playing field.

The ground covered here is multidisciplinary, with exploration into factors that are at play in the everyday working lives of all. Everyone interviewed brought with them their own expertise, experience, and views. They are uniquely their own, and each deserves as much space as the others. It is my hope that in showing some of the collective experiences of a subset of people who are remarkably similar across demographics but also wholly unique in how they see their shared experiences, we can highlight the areas where there is overlap in experience or views and see not only where there may be room for growth but also how far we have come. No one person was expected to have all the answers. There is no one correct way to navigate society's complex systems. Awareness is the first step to change, and while we have seen a lot of change in music, technology, and the advancement of women in many fields, we must maintain what we have gained and continue to look forward.

Some of the challenges are structural by country; in the case of childcare or health care, it will be a road of solutions and negotiations that society will travel together. Other challenges that are structural within the music industry, as in the case of pay, must be fought for in order for there to be just, fair, and timely payment—a solution that must be solved by and for the whole industry and something that unites us all. In other instances, it is up to the individual to choose how to authentically respond, whether the challenge is networking, mentoring, or navigating gatekeepers. Some have surpassed these barriers in their careers, while others are still working at surmounting them. To be aware of the challenges others face also gives us insight into how we can help one another as a whole and how the music being created might be affected. Music is a great place of community, a great place of creativity, of expression, and of innovation. There is no better place to come together than the global neighborhood that is music.

Everyone interviewed here brought their own ideas and experiences to the table, and it is hoped that, side-by-side, these ideas show a larger picture, one that everyone can find something to relate to, learn from, and carry forward. Allyship matters, as does mentorship and community. Visibility and representation are key. We need each other, and, equally, we need our allies to see us, remember us correctly, and hire us. Just because people are shaped by the societies they live in doesn't mean that we can't shape the music industry that we work and create in.

ACKNOWLEDGMENTS

First and foremost, thank you to the women who participated, giving me their time and their trust. I feel honored to have spoken with each of you about your experiences, and I keep hoping that there will be a day some time soon when we can all meet together in one place. Keep being the incredible people that you are, and keep recording, engineering, and producing all the music that you do.

I would also like to thank my teachers, all of whom have guided, inspired, and always believed in me. Thank you, each and every one, for always taking me seriously, for answering my million "But what does it sound like if . . . ?" questions, and for continuing to be inspiring.

Many thanks to all of my audio colleagues and peers the world over. You know who you are. I'd be nowhere without you, your pooled knowledge, your inspiration, and your friendship. Thank you to my many friends in music who also have been curious and supportive about this work. Thank you to every musician I've recorded and/or produced for trusting me with your music and sharing your artistic vision and journey with me. I am honored and humbled by your trust and artistry.

Thank you to the many musicians and bands who have inspired me in the first place to pick up a guitar, to play, to write, to record, to love music, and to pursue a life of music. There's no way possible to name all of you, but I wouldn't be here at all without the *music*.

Thank you: Russ Hepworth-Sawyer, Cody Darby (I guess you're the guy everyone has to thank in their book these days), Barkley McKay, Dr. Mark Marrington, Mark Burrows, Bill Edstrom (this wouldn't have happened without you!), Gary Gottlieb, Daniel Gumble, Jenny Bulcraig, Dr. Silvia Delerker and Zoe, Jason Kanter, Drew English, Rich Jensen, Dr. Ari Gratch, Danielle Montalvo, the "Zoom Brunch Crew," Dan and Ann Kilker, Mirette Seireg and Michael Levine and all at the MPath Music family, Boman Modine and Sara Garth, Jesse Lerner, Julia Pierce,

Benafsha Kaladjian, Andy Reynolds, Dom Smith, Martin Atkins (for all your invaluable advice, and the regular reminders to Get The Fuck Out Of Bed), Riane Eisler, Fenris Rupp, Heather Krantrowitz, Alex Choate, Sarah Jenkinson, Edith Denton, Maria Jardardottir, Greg Wands, Scott Wilzbach, the lovely folks at 2% Rising, Andrea Yankovsky, Kerry Pompeo, Suzy Reingold, Scott Overman, and all of my Patreon supporters, past and present—you've kept me alive more than you know. Thank you Twitterverse pals, I talk to so many of you daily. Thank you to so many of my friends (even if not listed here—forgive my overcrowded author brain) who listened to my doubts and anxieties, gave me a place to stay while I wrote this book during the pandemic, and helped get me out of my tiny apartment and into a better place to write. Thank you. Thank you.

REFERENCES

References proceeded by an asterisk (*) have been used as support material and have not been cited directly in the text.

Amos, Tori, and Ann Powers. 2005. *Piece by Piece; A Portrait of the Artist: Her Thoughts. Her Conversations.* New York: Broadway Books.

*Day, Jess. 2020. "What Do Toys Have to Do with Inequality?" *Let Toys Be Toys*, October 16. https://www.lettoysbetoys.org.uk/what-do-toys-have-to-do-with-inequality/.

*Erickson, Megan. 2011. "Where Are All the Women Scientists?" *Big Think*, September 27. https://bigthink.com/think-tank/where-are-all-the-women-scientists.

Faludi, Susan. 1991. *Backlash: The Undeclared War against American Women.* New York: Crown Publishers, Inc.

Fine, Cordelia. 2010. *Delusions of Gender: How Our Minds, Society, and Neurosexism Create Difference.* New York: W. W. Norton and Company.

Fine, Cordelia. 2017. *Testosterone Rex: Myths of Sex, Science, and Society.* New York: W. W. Norton and Company.

*Gittleson, Kim. 2017. "Where Are All the Women in Economics?" BBC.com, October 13. https://www.bbc.com/news/business-41571333.

Grey, Sarah. 2016. "Between a Boss and a Hard Place: Why More Women Are Freelancing." *BitchMedia*, August 2. https://www.bitchmedia.org/article/between-boss-and-hard-place-why-more-women-are-freelancing.

*Hepworth-Sawyer, Russ, Jay Hodgson, and Mark Marrington, eds. 2019. *Producing Music.* New York: Routledge.

*Hochschild, Arlie Russell, and Anne Machung. 1989. *The Second Shift: Working Parents and the Revolution at Home.* New York: Viking Penguin.

Hopper, Jessica. 2015. "The Invisible Woman: A Conversation with Björk." *Pitchfork*, January 21. https://pitchfork.com/features/interview/9582-the-invisible-woman-a-conversation-with-bjork/.

*Ignatius, Adi. 2013. "Where Are All the Women?" *Harvard Business Review*, April 4. https://hbr.org/2013/04/where-are-all-the-women.

Ingham, Tim. 2020. "Spotify Dreams of Artists Making a Living. It Probably Won't Come True." *Rolling Stone*, August 3. https://www.rollingstone.com/pro/features/spotify-million-artists-royalties-1038408/.

Jaffe, Eric. 2014. "The New Subtle Sexism toward Women in the Workplace." *Fast Company*, June 2. https://www.fastcompany.com/3031101/the-new-subtle-sexism-toward-women-in-the-workplace.

Kelan, Elizabeth. 2020. "Why Aren't We Making More Progress towards Gender Equity?" *Harvard Business Review*, December 21. https://hbr.org/2020/12/why-arent-we-making-more-progress-towards-gender-equity.

*Marcus, Ruth. 2017. "Where Are All the President's Women?" Opinion. *Washington Post*, September 15. https://www.washingtonpost.com/opinions/where-are-all-the-presidents-women/2017/09/15/f5bb1ff2-9a59-11e7-82e4-f1076f6d6152_story.html.

McIntyre, Phillip. 2008. "The Systems Model of Creativity: Analyzing the Distribution of Power in the Studio." *Journal of the Art of Record Production* 3 (November). https://www.arpjournal.com/asarpwp/the-systems-model-of-creativity-analyzing-the-distribution-of-power-in-the-studio/.

Saini, Angela. 2017. *Inferior: How Science Got Women Wrong—and the New Research That's Rewriting the Story*. Boston: Beacon Press.

Saujani, Reshma. 2016. "Teach Girls Bravery, Not Perfection." TED2016 Talk, February. https://www.ted.com/talks/reshma_saujani_teach_girls_bravery_not_perfection.

Schwartz, Barry. 2014. "The Way We Think about Work Is Broken." TED2014 Talk, Vancouver, BC, March. https://www.ted.com/talks/barry_schwartz_the_way_we_think_about_work_is_broken.

Schwartz, Barry. 2015. *Why We Work*. New York: TED Books, Simon and Schuster.

Science Museum. 2020. *Women in Computing*. Sciencemuseum.org, May 31. https://www.sciencemuseum.org.uk/objects-and-stories/women-computing.

*Solie, Ruth A., ed. 1993. *Musicology and Difference: Gender and Sexuality in Music Scholarship*. Berkeley and Los Angeles: University of California Press.

*Solnit, Rebecca. 2014. *Men Explain Things to Me*. Chicago: Haymarket Books.

Solnit, Rebecca. 2017. *The Mother of All Questions*. Chicago: Haymarket Books.

Sweet, Elizabeth V. 2015. "Beyond the Blue and Pink Toy Divide." TEDxUCDavis Talk, Davis, California, April. https://www.elizabethvsweet.com/tedx-talk.